Walking With

by Julian Richards

Dedication

I want to dedicate this book to my best friend and partner through life and ministry. My wife Wendy, who, for the last 37 years, has stood by me and so often held me up through all the ups and downs of life and ministry.

Thank you for walking with me and encouraging my walk with Jesus.

Dedication

Copyrights

Bible Versions quoted:

Introduction

When I was younger and in my first church, our pastor used to enjoy preaching about characters in the Bible. He loved looking at the life of someone in the Scriptures and consider how God dealt with him or her. One of his favourite ways of describing how he studied this was to say, 'I've been walking with ..... this week'.

This book is based on a series of messages I gave at the start of 2021 where I, too, 'walked with' the 12 Disciples of Jesus. One by one, week by week. This book looks at each of the Disciples in turn and seeks to tease out lessons for us today.

These men are a varied bunch of characters. Some we know loads about, others are all but unknown to us. This book focuses on the Biblical evidence and witness of the Bible, and not on any of the many church traditions which have developed.

I believe that Jesus chose each of the 12 for a reason, and that the information the gospels reveal will teach us something about them. Who were they? What can we learn from them? Why do we know more about some than we do about others? This book attempts to take a look at each Disciple in turn and think about these questions.

Where you see words in uppercase, this is for emphasis. Where I have quoted DIRECTLY from Scripture, the quotes are in *italics*. Where I am merely referencing it, they are not.

The word disciple is used in this book in two ways:

1. It is a descriptor of the 12 men Jesus chose.
2. It describes someone who might call themselves 'Christian'

As a mechanism to help the clarity of what I am writing, when I am referring to one of the 12, I will capitalise as 'Disciple'; otherwise I will use lower case. Except when quoting directly from Scripture, where I will retain the formatting of the text.

My prayer is that you will find much thought-provoking material here.

What is a disciple?

Before looking at the Disciples in turn, I feel it is first a wise move to look at what a disciple actually is. So, starting with the lists that the gospels give us of the Disciples, we read about who they were and what becoming a disciple actually entailed:

Matthew 10:1-4 — *"Jesus called his twelve disciples to him and gave them authority to drive out impure spirits and to heal every disease and sickness. These are the names of the twelve apostles: first, Simon (who is called Peter) and his brother Andrew; James son of Zebedee, and his brother John; Philip and Bartholomew; Thomas and Matthew the tax col-*

lector; James son of Alphaeus, and Thaddaeus; Simon the Zealot and Judas Iscariot, who betrayed him."

Mark 3:13-19 — "Jesus went up on a mountainside and called to him those he wanted, and they came to him. He appointed twelve that they might be with him and that he might send them out to preach and to have authority to drive out demons. These are the twelve he appointed: Simon (to whom he gave the name Peter), James son of Zebedee and his brother John (to them he gave the name Boanerges, which means "sons of thunder"), Andrew, Philip, Bartholomew, Matthew, Thomas, James son of Alphaeus, Thaddaeus, Simon the Zealot and Judas Iscariot, who betrayed him."

Luke 6:12-16 — "One of those days Jesus went out to a mountainside to pray, and spent the night praying to God. When morning came, he called his disciples to him and chose twelve of them, whom he also designated apostles: Simon (whom he named Peter), his brother Andrew, James, John, Philip, Bartholomew, Matthew, Thomas, James son of Alphaeus, Simon who was called the Zealot, Judas son of James, and Judas Iscariot, who became a traitor."

Interestingly, John's gospel doesn't list the disciples at all, but Luke also lists them a second time at the start of Acts:

Acts 1:13 — "When they arrived, they went upstairs to the room where they were staying. Those present were Peter, John, James and Andrew; Philip and Thomas, Bartholomew and Matthew; James son of Alphaeus and Simon the Zealot, and Judas son of James."

Looking at and comparing the lists, we can deduce that the Disciples are:

1. Simon Peter
2. Andrew (Simon Peter's brother)
3. James, son of Zebedee (Boanerges) and his brother
4. John, son of Zebedee (Boanerges)
5. Philip
6. Bartholomew, also understood to be Nathanael (John 1:45/John 21:2)
7. Thomas, also known as Didymus
8. Matthew the tax collector (or Levi. Luke 5)
9. James, son of Alphaeus (known as James the less)
10. Simon the Zealot
11. Judas, son of James / Thaddaeus
12. Judas Iscariot

These twelve men were Jews. They were un-educated[1] common people who gave up everything to be disciples of Christ. They lived with Jesus for three years, they accompanied Him as He travelled around performing signs and wonders, teaching and minister-ing to the people. They witnessed His discussions with the Pharisees and scribes, and they learned from Him. Though they didn't know it at the time, these men were chosen and being prepared by the Lord to take over and carry on the work He had started after His death and resurrection.

When we think of disciples today, we do tend to immediately think of these twelve men, the Disciples of Jesus. However, discipleship was not unusual at that time. It was not uncommon for teachers to gather around themselves a group of people to be their disciples. So, for example, we know that both John the Baptist AND the Pharisees had disciples (emphasis mine):

1. Mark 2:18, *'Now **John's disciples** and the Pharisees were fasting. Some people came and asked Jesus, 'How is it that **John's disciples** and the **disciples of the Pharisees** are fasting, but yours are not?"*
2. In Matthew 22:16, we read about how the Pharisees sent their disciples to Jesus to ask him a question to trap him: *'Then the Pharisees went out and laid plans to trap him in his words. They sent **their disciples** to him along with the Herodians.'*

That Jesus chose men to be His Disciples is not especially unusual, so if we are to really understand the relationships between Christ and the Disciples, our starting place is to talk generally about disciples and discipleship.

1. **Firstly**, A disciple is, 'one who learns'. Implications from this is that they recognise they have something to learn, AND they recognise that the teacher (Rabbi) has something to teach them.
2. **Secondly**, we must note that discipleship speaks to a relationship with a teacher and not adherence to an idea. In Jesus' day, you were never a disciple of a philosophy or idea, you were only ever the disciple of a teacher, a person, and you were expected to

follow his teaching and take on for yourself what he said. In a nutshell, you were to become like him. The concept that disciples become like their master would not be spelled out, it would not need to be, it would have been commonly understood in a way it is not today. I would not need to say any of what I am writing here to a first century Jew!

Here are some general implications of becoming a disciple …

Disciples wholeheartedly COMMIT to their master.

Disciples left their home and lived with their teacher, they followed him, and they were wholeheartedly committed to him. Luke 14:33 describes Jesus saying *'any one of you who does not renounce all that he has cannot be my disciple'*, and in His discussion with a rich man, He challenged him to sell all he has and to come and follow. In fact, He goes on to say, *'it is harder for a camel to go through the eye of a needle than it is for a rich man to enter the kingdom of heaven'* [2]. Setting aside arguments about Jesus meant when He said, 'the eye of a needle', we need to understand that the commitment Jesus expects of His disciples is TOTAL, not half-hearted commitment.

Malachi talks about the importance of whole-hearted commitment, as does Haggai, both of whom talk about it in the context of worship and how important it is in our walk.

Malachi talks of worship in terms of making promises to God and then not following through on them: *'Cursed is the cheat who has an acceptable male in his flock and vows to give it, but then sacrifices a blemished animal'*[3], he tells the people that God sees this as an act of contempt for him[4]. Haggai explains that the apparent unfruitfulness of the people is directly related to their neglect of worship: *'You expected much, but see, it turned out to be little. What you brought home, I blew away. Why?'* declares the LORD Almighty. *'Because of my house, which remains a ruin, while each of you is busy with your own house'*[5].

Jeremiah 12:2 says of the people in his day that God is *'always on their lips, but far from their hearts'*

A disciple is not someone who just says stuff and doesn't follow though on his words, he commits to following through with his actions. Jesus Himself says, *"why do you call me Lord and yet don't do what I say?"*[6]

But neither is a disciple someone who just does things to be seen by others. For show. Jesus says when we do that, we have already had our reward in full[7].

Paul described his piety before coming to faith in Christ, and says quite candidly that it was all worthless. In Philippians 3:4-8 he writes: *"I myself have reason for confidence in the flesh also. If anyone else thinks he has reason for confidence in the flesh, I have more: circumcised on the eighth day, of the people of Israel, of the tribe of Benjamin"* (the right background), *"a Hebrew of Hebrews; as to the law, a Pharisee"* (the right career and education) *"as to zeal, a persecutor of the church"* (the right ideology and worldview) *"as to righteousness under the law, blameless"* (can you get any more perfect than I was?) . *"But whatever gain I had, I counted as loss for the sake of Christ. Indeed, I count everything as loss because of the surpassing worth of knowing Christ Jesus my Lord."* Paul gave up everything, background, career, power, influence. He had everything people chase after, and when he measured them up against Christ, Paul says of them *"I count them as rubbish, in order that I may gain Christ"* [8]

Jesus alludes to this when he says *"Truly I tell you,"* Jesus said to them, *"no one who has left home or wife or brothers or sisters or parents or children for the sake of the kingdom of God will fail to receive many times as much in this age, and in the age to come eternal life."* [9]

So, a disciple of Christ is more than just someone who has believed in Him. It is someone who, having accepted the message of the good news, has surrendered their whole life to Him.

The rich man asked, *"what must I do to gain eternal life?"*, and Jesus responded, *"give up all your riches and follow me"* [10]. In other words, put ALL your trust in Jesus.

Putting your trust in Jesus reveals where your security is. Many people think all sorts of things will bring them security. They chase (for example):

1. Career
2. Possessions
3. Income
4. Pension pot
5. Status

Or even less material things, which ultimately do not bring eternal security either ...

1. Family, Children, Parents Etc
2. Ministry, good deeds, charitable works, altruism
3. Health

Trust in Jesus, REAL trust, says, "Whatever life throws at me, I will always trust in and rely on God".

Nowadays, news reports emerge from time to time of people who have been darlings of the modern ideology of the world changing their views and being completely savaged by the people they once championed. This is exactly what happened to Paul[11]. As our society careers headlong into godlessness, and hates and ridicules people of faith — especially those who follow Jesus, are you willing to give up status, reputation, career, even family for the sake of Him who gave up all for you?

Following Jesus may cost you EVERYTHING you have, and I'm not just talking about money or material possessions. In some parts of the world, you could find yourself being disinherited by family, sold into slavery, thrown into prison, tortured, or martyred. If you're a girl in some parts of the world, you could find yourself forcibly married to a grown man, this happens **today** in the 21st century. It puts the nasty comments on your social media stream or the risk of being de-platformed into context, doesn't it?

Disciples have counted the cost and are willing to pay it.

Disciples hold to the TEACHING of their master.

John 8:31 says, *'if you hold to my **teaching**, you really are my disciples'* (emphasis mine). Disciples were expected to hold to the teaching of their master, and more than that, they were learning to teach it themselves. 2 John 9 says if we do not continue in the teaching of Christ, we do not have God *'Everyone who does not abide in the teaching of Christ, does not have God. Whoever abides in the teaching has both the Father and the Son.'* I would say then that far from being an add-on, understanding the teaching of the Scriptures is foundational to our faith.

The description of the first church in Acts 2:42 clearly describes that the first believers were devoted to the apostle's teaching, and as Jesus said to the apostles what they were to teach was everything He commanded them, so the apostle's teaching IS Jesus' teaching:

Matthew 28:19-20 says, *"Therefore go and make disciples of all nations, baptising them in the name of the Father and of the Son and of the Holy Spirit, and **teaching** them to obey everything I have commanded you. And surely I am with you always, to the very end of the age."* (Note that the word "teaching" here is the Greek "διδάσκω" (didaskō), which means spoken teaching in the sense of lecturing)

Ezra is also described as "devoting" himself to the study of the Law — and to teaching it ... *"Ezra arrived in Jerusalem in the fifth month of the seventh year of the king. He had begun his journey from Babylon on the first day of the first month, and he arrived in Jerusalem on the first day of the fifth month, for the gracious hand of his God was on him. For Ezra had devoted himself to the study and observance of the Law of the Lord, and to **teaching** its decrees and laws in Israel."*[12]

Even when we follow Jesus, we are supposed to be learning. And as we do, we should always have an eye out for those we can pass on that learning. Deuteronomy 6:6-9 says: *"These commandments I give you today are to be upon your hearts. **Impress them on your children.** Talk about them when you walk along the road, when you lie down and when you get up. Tie them as symbols on your hands and bind them on your foreheads. Write them on the doorframes of your houses and on your gates."* Think of this: learn to walk and talk with Jesus during your day; wherever you are and whatever you're doing, as you move about, speak in your heart and your head with Jesus. Have a LIVING, MOVING and BREATHING relationship with Him!

In Romans 2:21 Paul says, *"you then, who teach others, do you not teach yourself?"* I would suggest that one critical function of the leadership is that of teaching, that of understanding the word of God, understanding His will and passing that knowledge on to the people in the church. Paul writes to Timothy (a young leader) and among other instructions tells him two things are important:

1. Firstly, to set an example in life[13],
2. Secondly, to devote himself to public reading of Scripture and to preaching and teaching [14].

It is interesting that in the UK, and USA (and I suspect all over the Christian world), churches, when looking for a pastor, ask him or her to come and preach. But they don't usually ask them to spend time visiting or doing the practical things around the church. I would suggest that practical tasks are not primarily the domain of the elders, but the domain of the deacons. It is not without reason that the apostles say: *"It would not be right for us to neglect the ministry of the word of God in order to wait on tables. Brothers and sisters, choose seven men from among you who are known to be full of the Spirit and wisdom. We will turn this responsibility over to them and will give our attention to prayer and the ministry of the word."* [15]

Whose teaching was actually being followed? It was the teaching of Jesus. The apostles taught what Jesus had taught them. Jesus taught that the Father sent Him; He said, *"I do not speak on my own, but only what the father tells me"* [16], and He told the disciples *"teaching them everything I have commanded you"* [17].

I can imagine the first believers asking the Apostles to tell stories of the master...

- "Tell us about when Jesus ...."
- "Tell us again the stories Jesus told, and how He told you what they mean"
- "explain to us again how Jesus fulfils the messianic prophecies"
- "tell again the story of His death and resurrection"

Theology is not dry and dusty, it is vital and life giving. We all want to get to know our Saviour and our God better (at least I assume that if you call yourself a Christian, you do). We can find him and get to know him better in the words of the Bible. Furthermore, we will find all we need for life and righteousness in its pages, and not in philosophies or systems. In it, you will read and hopefully understand God's heart, His plan for the world, the story of his chosen people and the life of His son.

The apostle's teaching was a vibrant, experienced understanding of our Lord and how He lived among them. It was their testimony, and we have passages like Revelation 12:11 to remind us of how powerful our testimony is.

Disciples seek to BECOME like their master.

Disciples were expected to become like their master. In fact, if they weren't like their master, they weren't regarded as true disciples.

Luke 6:40 says, *"A disciple is not above his teacher, but everyone when he is fully trained **will be like** his teacher".* (ESV)

Matthew 10:25 says, *"It is enough for the disciple **to be like** his teacher, and the servant like his master."* (ESV)

Our actions reveal who our master is. Jesus says to the Jews in John 8:44, *"You are of your father the devil, and your will is to do your father's desires. He was a murderer from the beginning, and does not stand in the truth, because there is no truth in him. When he lies, he speaks out of his own character, for he is a liar and the father of lies"* but in John 14:12, he says *"whoever believes in me will do the works I have been doing, and they will do even greater things than these, because I am going to the Father".*

Jesus says to the Jewish leaders in John 5:19 *"the Son can do nothing by himself; he can do only what he sees his Father doing, because whatever the Father does, the Son also does".*

Our model Jesus says He only does what the Father does, and if we are to follow Him effectively, we are to be like Him. What does that mean? Jesus gave us an example in John 13 when He washes the disciples feet. At the end of it, He asks if they understand what He has done [18], and explains that *"Now that I, your Lord and*

Teacher, have washed your feet, you also should wash one an-
other's feet. I have set you an example that you should do as I
have done for you." [19].

The Bible talks about becoming conformed to the image of God's son[20]. Paul talks in 1 Corinthians 15:49 of us bearing the image of Christ *"just as we have borne the image of the earthly man, so shall we bear the image of the heavenly man"* and in 2 Corinthians 3:18 he says *"we all, who with unveiled faces contemplate the Lord's glory, are being transformed into his image"*. John also picks up on this image and writes, *"what we will be has not yet been made known. But we know that when Christ appears, we shall be like him"*[21]

Romans 12:2 gives us a hint as to HOW. Just as Jesus speaks of the real person being not in his actions, but in his inner man, Paul says we will be transformed by the *"renewing of our minds"*. This tells us that the process of filling our minds with the knowledge of God not only brings us closer to 'Christ-like-ness', but Paul goes on to say that obedience to that knowledge aligns us with the perfect will of God: *"Then you will be able to test and approve what God's will is, "his good, pleasing and perfect will."* The deeper our knowledge of Christ, the deeper our understanding of Him, and the more like Him we become. We get to know Jesus in the pages of our Bibles.

Of course, knowledge alone will not produce a Christlike character. The knowledge we gain from God's Word must impact our hearts and convict us of the need to obey what we have learned.

The natural consequence of knowing and obeying God is that He becomes greater and greater, while we become less and less as we yield more control of our lives to him. Just as John the Baptist knew that *"he* (Jesus) *must increase, but I must decrease"* [22], so the Christian grows to reflect more of Christ and less of his own nature. Luke sums it up best when he describes what Jesus told His disciples: *"If anyone would come after me, he must deny himself and take up his cross daily and follow me. For whoever wants to save his life will lose it, but whoever loses his life for me will save it"* [23]. The cross was an instrument of death, and Jesus encourages us to take up our cross and put to death our old sin nature upon it. God wants us to forget about this world and all its temporary pleasures and be obedient to His Word. Jesus is the living Word[24], and the Bible is God's written Word. Therefore, conforming to the Word of God is conforming to Christ.

The New Testament is full of references to our becoming like Christ (here are just a few)....

- Romans 8:29 tells us, *"those God foreknew he also predestined to be conformed to the image of his Son, that he might be the firstborn among many brothers and sisters."*
- 1 Corinthians 15:49, *"just as we have borne the image of the earthly man"*(Adam), *so shall we bear the image of the heavenly man"*(Christ).
- 2 Corinthians 3:18, *"And we all, who with unveiled faces contemplate the Lord's glory, are **being trans-***

formed into his image with ever-increasing glory, which comes from the Lord, who is the Spirit."
- Philippians 3:20-21, *"But our citizenship is in heaven. And we eagerly await a Saviour from there, the Lord Jesus Christ, who, by the power that enables him to bring everything under his control,* **will transform our lowly bodies so that they will be like his glorious body***".*
- 1 John 3:2, *"we know that when Christ appears,* **we shall be like him***, for we shall see him as he is."*

What does that look like?

1. It is revealed in our behaviour. Supremely shown in Christ's example of servanthood, the passage in John's gospel which I've already read says *"Now that I, your Lord and Teacher, have washed your feet, you also should wash one another's feet. I have set you an example that you should do as I have done for you".* [25] ... and ...
2. It is revealed in our attitude. Paul says to the Philippians [26] that our attitudes should be the same as that of Christ Jesus: *"You must have the same attitude that Christ Jesus had"* and he spells out what that looks like: *"like-minded, having the same love, being one in spirit and of one mind. Do nothing out of selfish ambition or vain conceit. Rather, in humility value others above yourselves, not looking to your own interests but each of you to the interests of the others".*

And finally, this might all seem a bit much, but Jesus has a great promise for us:

Matthew 11:28-30: *"Come to me, all you who are weary and burdened, and I will give you rest. Take my yoke upon you and learn from me, for I am gentle and humble in heart, and you will find rest for your souls. For my yoke is easy and my burden is light."*

When Jesus spoke of the bread of life in John 6, He challenges the people who were following Him and says: *"Very truly I tell you, you are looking for me, not because you saw the signs I performed but because you ate the loaves and had your fill. Do not work for food that spoils, but for food that endures to eternal life, which the Son of Man will give you. For on him God the Father has placed his seal of approval."*[27]

In other words, they were chasing him for what they could get out of him, but that stuff doesn't last. What lasts is doing what God has called us to do, which he goes on to say is *"to believe in the one he has sent."*[28].

Is our faith about US? Or about HIM?, do we belong to the crowd of people who are only following Jesus for what they can get out of it?

The thing is that if that is the case, we will abandon our faith when things get tough.

Jesus turns to the 12 and asks, *"are you going to leave me too?"* and Peter's response sums up our confession of faith ... *"Lord, to whom shall we go? You have the words of eternal life. We have come to believe and to know that you are the Holy One of God."* [29]

Here is a question for you to ponder: Am I a disciple of Jesus or just a follower in the crowd?

1. Simon Peter

The disciple named first in every list is Simon Peter. Not only do the accounts of Peter we find in the Gospels seem to resonate with people, which tends to make them memorable, we have more of them. There are 176 direct references to him alone in the New Testament!

Peter's life, his interactions with Jesus, and the role he played in the first church in Acts could be a book all of its own. So I am only going to pick one or two cherries off this particular tree for us to suck on!

Firstly, here are some basic facts about Peter to put him in some kind of context. According to the synoptic[30] Gospels, Jesus' first encounter with Peter is on the shores of the Sea of Galilee, and although they don't specify WHERE exactly they first met, John does say that Peter was from the town of Bethsaida which is a town on the shores of the sea of Galilee. Peter is a Galilean and his accent is strong[31].

Accents are funny things, aren't they? They define where we are from. British accents are so very varied, and despite our parents correcting our accents as children, most people are identifiable by them. Where I live, in the UK, very few people speak with what is called "received pronunciation" (informally known as "Queen's English"), and although it's not so marked now, as when I was younger, Queen's English is still considered by many to be an indication that you are educated and if you retain a strong regional accent the unspoken assumption was that you are not. Interestingly, like the assumptions of those people today, the same thing was true in first century Palestine. Peter's Galilean accent would have been recognisable, reveal his origins and suggest that he was not educated [32]. We read something of this in Acts 4:13: *"When they* (the Sanhedrin) *saw the courage of Peter and John and realised that they were unschooled, ordinary men, they were astonished"*.

Peter has two names, Simon and Peter. Or more properly, Simeon and Cephas, Simeon being a Hebrew name and Cephas an Aramaic one. Simeon/Simon is the name he was known by before his encounter with Jesus. It was, presumably, the name given to him by his parents. Cephas (or its Greek counterpart Petros) is the name which was given to him by Jesus himself and dominates NT usage. Petros means "rock".

It is not uncommon to find the names Simon and Peter "coupled" as Simon Peter, but for clarity here I will refer to him as Peter, even if I'm describing events recorded before Jesus changes his name, otherwise it could get confusing as his name would otherwise flit backward and forward depending on which Bible passage I'm referencing.

Things Peter is known for...

1. He was part of a small group of disciples who are really close to Jesus. An "inner circle" (if you will) of Peter, James & John. They were regularly mentioned in situations where the others were not present.
2. Peter was the disciple who walked on the water, the one who had the desire to walk on the water and the courage to try.
3. Peter was impulsive. We often read of him saying things first, or saying something without thinking and then regretting what he said. He sometimes DID get it right, for example it was Peter whose confession of Jesus as the Christ is commended by Jesus as coming directly from God.
4. Peter was a "Doer". He was not one to hang back and let others take the strain. It is Peter who cut off the servant's ear in the garden of Gethsemane.
5. Peter denied Jesus 3 times. When Jesus is arrested, actually ALL the disciples[33] ran away, but we are given extra information about Peter. We are told the specifics about his denials.
6. Peter was one of the key leaders in the early church. It was Peter who preached the very first post resurrection evangelistic message on the day of pentecost, recorded at the beginning of Acts.
7. Peter's name is given to 2 of the epistles (unsurprisingly, 1 & 2 Peter). Whether he actually wrote them is the subject of some disagreement. My own feeling

is that on balance I think he probably did, but this
book is not the place for such study.

8. Tradition has it that he was crucified upside down
   (Foxes book of Martyrs) because he didn't consider
   himself worthy to be crucified like his Lord was.

Family.

We also know something of Peter's family circumstances:

1. We know who his father was, he is described as
   "Son of John", [34] otherwise known as Jonah. [35].
2. We know he had a brother, Andrew, who also became one of the disciples. (John 1:44; Mark 1:16;
   Luke 5:2; John 21:3).
3. Peter was married. Two references tell us this, Mark
   1:29–31 mentions his Mother–in–Law. And in 1 Corinthians 9:5 Peter's wife is cited as an example by
   Paul because Peter took her with him when he went
   on ministry.
4. Peter's home was initially in Bethsaida [36]. Though it
   is likely (probable even) that at some point he
   moved to Capernaum as Mark 1:21ff, records that
   after speaking in the Synagogue in Capernaum, Jesus and the disciples went straight to Peter's house,
   so either Bethsaida is quite close to Capernaum OR
   (which I think more likely) he had moved there.

Here are a few points I think are worth considering.

The letting down of nets.

This is the account of how Peter fished all night, he caught nothing and after coming back to shore empty-handed, with no catch, is told by Jesus to put his nets down again. This happens not once, but twice. Firstly, at the start of his ministry (which I will concentrate on). Secondly, it happens at the end of the Gospel narrative where the risen Jesus did the same thing again, and it is in this that Peter recognises Jesus. This speaks to how much this had imprinted on Peter the first time.

So, we read of a situation where Peter, the "professional" does what Jesus the "amateur" tells him to do, and a miracle follows.

Whenever you have a problem, it seems like everyone suddenly becomes an expert in that field. Before I became a pastor, I worked in the property profession as an estate agent and surveyor, and it seemed like everyone I knew thought they were experts and regularly offered me advice on how to sell houses. This encounter it is like that. A carpenter's son is telling a fisherman how to fish.

When Jesus tells Peter to put down the nets again I wonder if Peter felt like I did when people whose knowledge was based on one house sale only, seemed to think they knew more than I did and that I needed their advice when my knowledge was based on years of training and working through the technicalities of my caseload which over a decade in the business amounted to probably many thousands of different transactions.

Peter's response to Jesus shows that these conditions are not right for fishing, they'd not caught anything all night. But these are no ordinary circumstances. So despite all appearances and, I'm convinced, Peter's better judgement, he let down the nets again. This is a great example of faith despite recent experience (a fishless night) Peter let down the net and his faith was rewarded with success. So much so that it nearly turns to disaster, a sinking boat!!!

Our experiences and our present circumstances may tell us that there is no point in acting or doing that particular thing we feel God is asking us to do, yet we need to get to the place where despite what reason seems to be saying (it'll never work) we nevertheless do what our Lord asks. The result, I believe, will be equally successful, and possibly just as miraculous!

When the fish are landed, Peter realises that this is no ordinary man!!! In fact, so much so, that his response is one that echoes the responses of Isaiah & Jeremiah[37]. He falls at Jesus feet and confesses his unworthiness. Jesus doesn't call those who think they are worthy. In fact, those who thought they were worthy were the Pharisees, and Jesus had some forceful things to say about them. He calls them hypocrites and whitewashed tombs. The Bible says that man looks at the outward appearance, but that God looks at the heart [38].

So many people in the Bible used by God would be rejected if they used their own assessments of their own abilities to follow his guidance ...

1. Moses, the stutterer, is used to speak to pharaoh, the most powerful man in his time.
2. Gideon, the coward hiding in a wine press, is used to raise an army to fight the Midianites.
3. Paul, the persecutor of Christians, is used to carry the gospel message to the world.
4. Rahab, the gentile prostitute, is used to save the Israelite spies and becomes part of the line of Christ.
5. David, the adulterous murderer, is used by God to pen some of the most beautiful worship which has endured for millennia.
6. Jeremiah, the youth, is used to speak God's truth to an entire generation.
7. The disciples, ordinary flawed men are chosen by Jesus to be his disciples, to proclaim his gospel (note: NOT the priests, not the "religious" people, not the "good" people).

I could go on, but you get the point ... Our experiences and assessments of ourselves, of what we can and cannot do, are irrelevant when it comes to the calling of God on our lives. It seems to me that too often we look at such things to determine whether or not we can do what God is calling to, instead of looking at God and trusting that if **He** calls us, we can do it. Here are some examples for us to consider:

- I meet many people who feel inadequate because they didn't do well at school, they feel that somehow things they did (or rather didn't) do at school disqualifies them in some way from some ministry not other.
- Or, do you think you are not the right age? That you're too old, or too young? Don't buy into this nonsense that age is a factor that contributes to whether God uses you or not! Abraham was 75 when God called him, David was anointed by Samuel when he was about 13 (but he was nearly 40 before he actually became king). Samuel himself was only just weaned when he first heard from God. Josiah was 8 when he became king, Moses was about 80 when God called him. Simeon and Anna at the temple when Jesus was presented were both elderly, and were used by God to prophecy over him. When they were called, the disciples' ages could have been anything in the range from mid-teens to early 40s, Paul wrote to Timothy_ "don't let anyone look down on you because you are young" _[39], John was elderly when God gave him the vision of heaven that we know as Revelation written around AD95 John is at least in his 70s, which in that culture and at that time was exceptionally old. So if you're in what we might call your golden years, or if you are still regarded as a child, don't buy the lie that your usefulness to God is defined by your age.

You might think you don't have the right background or upbringing, that you come from the wrong place and have the wrong accent, that there is something in your past or family environment which disqualifies you from His service, or some perception that you should have had the same experience as someone who is serving God, and because you haven't, it clearly means you're not as gifted / skilled / called as they are. But remember:

- Gideon was the 'least' in the smallest family in the smallest tribe [40]
- Jephthah was a half brother (and by a prostitute)[41], he was driven out and told he had no place in the family and would not share the inheritance. Yet, God used him.
- Jesus was from Nazareth and as Nathanael says:_ "Nazareth? Can anything good come from there?"_ [42]

The Good News for us is that God doesn't listen to the opinions of others. He doesn't look at our pedigree, our past performance (either our failures or our successes), He doesn't take references, or give probationary periods before deciding whether or not you are useful in the Kingdom and confirming your appointment as His ambassador! God's track record is one of choosing things that 'are not' (or, perhaps, 'not much' or 'not yet') and making them into something[43]. God chose a nation before it was even born, He chose prophets before they were born (he says this to both Jeremiah in Jeremiah 1:5 AND to Isaiah in Isaiah 49:1).

Jesus chose a rag tag motley bunch of misfits, named them Disciples, and with them turned the world upside down! He knows what we were like.

What God thinks of you and whether or not he decides to use you is not dependent on you, your past, your skills or even your gifting, it is entirely up to The Lord whom He chooses.

1 Corinthians 1:26-28 says this (and I find this really encouraging!) *"Brothers and sisters, think of what you were when you were called. Not many of you were wise by human standards; not many were influential; not many were of noble birth. But God chose the foolish things of the world to shame the wise; God chose the weak things of the world to shame the strong. God chose the lowly things of this world and the despised things—and the things that are not—to nullify the things that are."*

If you are carrying something that you think is a block to the power of God working through you, you need to understand that this is something that God is already aware of, yet He chooses you anyway!

I love the meme which says "God already factored in my stupidity when he called me"!!

Peter is often a representative of those around him

Peter often spoke as a representative of the disciples, and asked the questions they were all thinking...

- In Mark 8:29 Peter responds to a question which is asked of all the disciples (*"who do you say that I am?"*)
- Matthew 15:15 Peter is the one to ask about the explanation of the Parable.
- Luke 12:41 It is Peter who asks if the parable about watchfulness is for everyone or just the disciples.

These are just three examples.

Peter stands in a long line of representatives...

1. Abraham pleads for Sodom [44]
2. Moses represents the People of God before Pharaoh [45]
3. Esther represents the Jews before the king [46]

Supremely, this is what Christ did for us.

1. Isaiah 53:4,5_ "He was pierced for **our** transgressions"_
2. 1 Peter 2:24 *"He, himself, bore **our** sins"*
3. Galatians 3:13_ "Christ became a curse **for us**"_

Paul tells us that this is one of the ministries we have, which is to plead and bring reconciliation between man and God.

2 Corinthians 5:18 *"all this is from God, who reconciled us to Himself through Christ and gave us the ministry of reconciliation: that God was reconciling the world to Himself in Christ, not counting men's sins against them. And He has committed to us the message of reconciliation."*

One of the most important things we can do is to stand in the gap between man and God. When we pray for those around us, we plead to God on their behalf and we are standing in the gap for them. When we evangelise, and get involved in talking to people and witnessing, we are representing God to them.

But there's more to this. I believe a very significant event is recorded in Acts 15:1-21, which describes an event in the lives of Paul and Barnabas. The gospel was spreading to gentile believers, and this was causing disagreement. Note v2 describes it as a 'sharp dispute'! (a ROW) I believe this issue had the potential to split the church right in two, and it is Peter who defended the Gentile believers. It is this action that I believe held the church together at this point.

Interestingly, Paul and Barnabas stand side by side at the Jerusalem council advocating for the gentile believers and very soon afterwards they part company because Barnabas wanted to give John Mark a second chance, but Paul didn't. Barnabas stood in the gap again, and they disagreed so strongly, they fell out and parted company [47].

In the book of Philemon, Paul is doing a similar thing. He is standing in the gap between a master and his runaway slave, pleading for him.

When we see conflict arising, we can take a number of actions...

1. We can take sides. Usually, the side we take is coloured by our experiences, beliefs and feeling towards the parties involved.
2. We can stand back and avoid the conflict altogether. We can let them slug it out themselves. Or
3. We can stand in the gap and try to bring peace and resolution.

Which stance did Jesus commend? Well, *"Blessed are the peacemakers, for they will be called children of God."* [48]

We have a challenge here, not to jump in with both feet when we are witnessing or being told about a disagreement or conflict, but to do what we can to bring about reconciliation and peace.

To conclude this section, just a couple of questions to think about...

1. Do I stand in the gap and try to bring peace between God and my friends?
   - By coming to Him in prayer on their behalf
   - By representing Him to them in my witness
2. Am I a person who is willing to stand in the gap between people?

Just as Peter stood in the Gap between the Jewish and Gentile believers, when we witness conflict or threat of conflict, do we take sides? Do we avoid the situation all together and hope "it'll blow over," or do we try to be peacemakers?

Peter asks about and learns first hand the power of forgiveness

This is connected to the previous point, because forgiveness is so often a pre-requisite for peace. Or to put it another way, unforgiveness will all too frequently sabotage attempts to bring peace. Forgiveness is foundational to peace with my brother and peace in my own spirit.

Start with Matthew 18:21 *"Then Peter came to Jesus and asked, "Lord, how many times shall I forgive my brother or sister who sins against me? Up to seven times?"*

We cannot walk with Peter without being confronted by the issue of forgiveness. Look back to the gospels: Peter had a very chequered history with Jesus (he only used to open his mouth to change foot!). We read him saying to Jesus: *"even if all of these leave you Lord, I won't, even if it means death!"* [49]. Yet, we read on and see that on 3 separate occasions, Peter denies Jesus, even to the point of calling down a curse on himself. Can you imagine what kind of internal problems this would have created in Peter? The guilt, the shame he would have felt. I guess the time after Jesus' death and before the resurrection would have been a very difficult time for Peter, who promised so much but delivered so little. Peter must have had a real sense of failure and disappointment within: "I've really blown it — what if this happens again, Lord? What if I let you down again?"

I believe many of us struggle with this. We live with a sense of failure because at some point in the past we've fallen short, we think we're hypocrites because we've not followed through on our claims with our actions.

We look at the verse in Matthew that says, *"if anyone denies me before men, I will deny him before my father in heaven"* 50. We think that's it — I've blown it. I know lots of Christians who have not specifically denied Jesus, but have nevertheless allowed pressure from outside to weaken their witness, and as a result, they live under a dreadful sense of guilt and fear that they have fallen foul of this statement. This creates a huge frontier that God needs to deal with. We wonder — can He?

Look the account of Peter. Isn't this the very thing that Peter did? Do we believe that Peter will be denied before God by Jesus? Don't we rather believe that Peter received forgiveness and restoration from the Lord?

I believe that when we read John 21, we see Jesus dealing directly with this very issue, it is not a coincidence that Jesus says *"do you love me more than these?"* when he's talking to Peter, I believe it's a reminder that Peter said_ "even if these leave you I won't"_ 51. Neither is it a coincidence that Jesus challenges Peter three times, which parallels and (I'm sure) reminds Peter of his three denials. Then, Jesus echoes some of the very first words he ever spoke to Peter. In their first interaction, Jesus told Peter to follow Him [52]. Then after Jesus' resurrection, and at the special breakfast on the shore where Jesus restored Peter, His last recorded words to him were once again, *"follow me!"* [53]. Peter is reminded of that start, he is restored in his relationship with Christ, and recommissioned in his calling.

It seems that in that moment, Jesus addressed an internal frontier in Peter, which enabled him to receive the blessing of the Holy Spirit and preach such a sermon on the day of Pentecost.

The truth is that if you have at some point found yourself in that position. You may not even necessarily have denied Jesus, but you kept quiet about your faith when you know you ought to have spoken out. There is forgiveness, restoration and peace available to you today. **YOU HAVE NOT BLOWN IT**!

Peter's failure doesn't cancel his identity.

Once a decision to follow Jesus is made, He becomes our identity. We are then Christ followers. This identity trumps our last name, our role at work, or the club, our position in the family, our economic status or any other human measure we use to assess ourselves. We have been made as His image bearers, we are members of His family, a part of the nation of God. We are His ambassadors, following His example and representing Him before the people around us. This is a spiritual reality for us, whether or not we understand it or live by it.

In John 21 when Jesus reinstated Peter, He reminded him of his identity, He reminded him of what was the most important thing about him — his belonging to God.

Jesus reminded Peter of his identity and importance in Matthew 16:18, *"And I say also unto thee, That thou art Peter, and upon this rock, I will build my church, and the gates of hell shall not prevail against it."* The name Peter means 'a rock or stone' Jesus knew the destiny of Peter.

I am so grateful for my identity in Christ, and I am just as thankful that He forgives me when I mess up. Our relationship with Christ should mature, and we should gain strength in combating the world and its pitfalls. But how sweet it is that when we do fail, our Lord loves us enough to look into our eyes and tell us again to follow him. We must all understand that our identity is found in Christ. It is not found in our actions or behaviour (which incidentally is why it not our behaviour which saves us).

Paul says in Ephesians 1:13-14, *"you also were included in Christ when you heard the message of truth, the gospel of your salvation. When you believed, you were marked in him with a seal, the promised Holy Spirit, who is a deposit guaranteeing our inheritance until the redemption of those who are God's possession — to the praise of his glory."*

So, what does Peter teach us?

1. That our expertise, our failures, our experiences, our talents, valuable though they are, do not impact on God's love of us, nor do they add to our salvation in any way. That the presence or lack of particular skill, experience or attribute neither qualifies nor disqualifies us from God's call on our lives.
2. That we are called to represent the King of kings and the Lord of lords before a watching world.
3. That there is a way back from our failures of faith, whatever they are, if we will come to Christ and allow Him to minister to us.

Now that is Good news!

2. Andrew

Next we come to the disciple called Andrew. Andrew is Simon Peter's brother, and is so overshadowed by him that we know surprisingly little about him.

Most of what we know about Andrew comes from the account at the beginning of John's gospel, [54] where Andrew and John are told by John the Baptist that Jesus is the Lamb of God, and they follow Him. They stay with Jesus all day and after that encounter, Andrew goes and gets his brother Simon, and brings him to Jesus. Other than this and his inclusion in the lists of the disciples, there are only one or two passing references to him in the gospels, so for example it is Andrew who found the boy with the loaves and fishes that Jesus uses to feed 5,000 people [55], and it is Andrew who was approached by Philip and asked to introduce some gentiles to Jesus [56]. And that's about it.

I have a brother. He is older than I am, he is louder than I am, he is wittier and quicker than I am, and in our family gatherings, he seems to be able to command the attention of people in a way that I am just not able to, and when I am around my brother, I feel pushed into the background, pushed into taking a back seat and living under his shadow. I really identify with Andrew because it seems to me that he also lived most of his life under the shadow of his much more prominent and dynamic brother.

So, what can we learn from this relatively unknown disciple?

Andrew was faithful in the shadows

Unlike Barnabas, and unlike John the Baptist, who both had roles of leadership and prominence and chose to allow another to become more prominent and to take a back seat, Andrew was never prominent in the first place.

It seems to me that many, far too many people believe that the most valuable place of ministry is in places of leadership and at the front, and they either forget or they don't realise that ministry happens now, where you are — not where you aspire to be. Very few people are called to what might be described as a prominent ministry. For the vast majority of us, following God and being used by Him happens in the shadows, it goes unnoticed by the world at large.

This is true even for those who are pastors and worship leaders and church leaders. With the exception of a handful of men and women, the huge majority of church leaders will also live out their lives in relative obscurity, and will be forgotten by history within a very short space of time.

And that's how it should be.

A belief that effectiveness for God only happens in prominent positions does a number of things...

1. **It creates an atmosphere of competition**. There is an account of David and Saul, we read in 1 Samuel 18:6-9 that women came out from all the towns in Israel after David had killed the Philistine and sang this: *"Saul has slain his thousands, and David his tens of thousands."* Saul was king, he should have had a prime place in the hearts (and the songs) of his subjects, and the bible records that this event made Saul so angry that *"from that time on Saul kept a close eye* [57] *on David."*

The disciples also fell into this trap, they argued about who would be the greatest among them [58], and in 2,000 years things don't seem to have moved on much! Many people in churches who want to be effective strive and compete with one another for the preaching spots, or the leading worship spots. I noticed this very much when I was training for the ministry. It seemed that the whole class was a competition, who preached best on Sunday? Who had the best response? Who led worship best, or had the most effective children's talk? But Jesus says something very significantly different to the narrative the world promotes. Jesus says this: *"the greatest among you should be like the youngest, and the one who rules like the one who serves"* [59], He modelled it for the disciples in the upper room, He said *"I am among you as the one who serves"* [60]. That's our blueprint. His life is the blueprint for our lives. We must follow it and no other. We must reject all other blueprints drawn by our pride, or envy, or selfishness. When we do that, we start using our gifts, our skills our talents, even our strength for others rather than to promote ourselves, it is a better way to live. Better for the church, better for others and counter-intuitively, better for us as well.

2. **It discourages ministry where we are**. If we think that ministry happens only in situations where we are 'up front', and that God works in those situations more powerfully, it can create a belief that unless we are like Billy Graham or some other larger than life Christian we know, then ministry is not our role, that we must be content with nothing. Unless we throw away the idea that we have to somehow get into some kind of position before we can really be effective, we will always be looking to the future and not ministering where we are. I know the context is slightly different, but when Moses was questioning his ability to do what God had called him to do, God said, *"what have you got in your hand?"*[61]. We so often dismiss what is right in front of our eyes because we don't think it's enough, but when surrendered to God, even the smallest thing becomes potent, powerful and effective. It may be in the form of your talents, skills, gifting, potential, wealth or other resources. God knows you, and He knows what you have in your hands. The Bible is actually filled with many like Moses who were asked the same question; The loaves and fishes which were not enough to feed the people were handed over to Jesus who multi-

plied it, and they could feed over 5 thousand people and still have some left over, 12 baskets full of food to be precise. In 2 Kings 4:2, all a widow had was a jar of oil. A jar of oil surrendered to God was enough to pay the debt owed by her late husband. She gave it up, God multiplied it, and she had enough left over to live on with her sons. God can multiply your little, so why don't you surrender what you have, and sit back and see what only He can do with it?

3. **It encourages pride and arrogance**. What this does is create a danger that we see the ministry, the prominence itself as the important thing, and elevates those who do it to a status they should never have. This in turn can lead to people falling. It is not for nothing that Proverbs 16:18 says *"Pride goes before destruction, a haughty spirit before a fall."* James 4:6 tells us that *"God opposes the proud, but shows favour to the humble"*. A belief that in order to be effective for God means that we have to strive to be important, and that those who are important are somehow more useful to God creates in us a tendency to measure people up against each other and lose focus on ourselves and our responsibility to follow the leading of God.

Andrew saw the value of the insignificant

One thing about being in the limelight is that you tend to start to be focused on the big things. You start to think you are important and to treat others differently.

It has been said that you can measure the stature of a man not by how he treats his superiors or even his equals, but by how he treats his subordinates, how he values those who serve Him.

It was Andrew who found a small boy with 5 loaves and two fishes in the account of the feeding of the 5,000. Would this boy have been overlooked if Andrew had not seen the invisible? We can never know that, but I suspect the answer might be "yes". We must always be aware that God will often choose the insignificant things and the "little people" to accomplish his purposes.

Likewise, we must also remember that those small, insignificant acts which we do in the name of Christ are the most powerful. God more frequently speaks to people through small acts of kindness, rather than through grand gestures, which actually tend to draw attention to the one making the gesture. I would suggest that He prefers it this way.

The "small" of the loaves and fishes echoes the "small" of the widow's offering.

We think that we do not have the resources to help people. We're right. In 1985, a number of famous bands and rock stars got together and put on an event called "Live Aid", which is estimated to have raised more than

£150 million pounds. Way beyond any resource a church would be able to raise. The point? To bring aid to the poorest people in the world. There are other efforts as well now, we have sport aid, comic relief, children in need and other efforts by the rich the famous and the important to fundraise for the poor, between them raising many millions of pounds every year. But if we pause and look at the world, consider this: it has been decades since that first Live Aid concert, and what difference has it made? We STILL see images of poverty in those places despite the efforts of those events.

It seems that Jesus was right when He said, *"the poor will always be with you"* [62]. Since that first Live Aid concert, many hundreds and thousands of Christians have gone to the poor all over the world and lived among the people, they have loved them and ministered to them, they have funded themselves largely through other Christians giving just a few pounds here and a few pounds there. Many come home because they just cannot raise the support they need. They often minister in countries which are hostile to their faith and in the face of criticism from secular people back home making accusations of cultural imperialism (interestingly those same people would support the establishing of democracy overseas).

They are the unsung heroes, they are the ones the TV cameras will never visit, they are the ones who give of their own resources, they sacrifice comfort and careers and families and friendships (which are so often dependent on proximity to flourish) and even health. And no one notices. Except God.

The next thing I believe we can learn from Andrew is this:

Andrew has an "introduction ministry" or "a gift of invitation"

Andrew meets with Jesus. He is already a disciple of John the Baptist and follows Jesus because of what John the Baptist said. We then read that he spends the day with Jesus and then goes home to his brother Simon and brings him to Jesus.

Witness should come from personal experience

You can hear about something whether it is as mundane as a football match, or as exciting as a miracle from three different sources...

a. Someone who has heard or read about it.
b. Someone who watched it as it happened.
c. Someone who was a participant.

In a court of law, an eyewitness can testify, but second hand evidence has no value. It is deemed hearsay and dismissed. Only those who actually witnessed an event are asked to testify. The ones of whom most notice is taken are the participants themselves.

Matthew 28:6 says: *"Come and see the place where he lay. Then go quickly and tell his disciples."* The impact of the resurrection is found not in second hand testimony, but in eyewitness and participant testimony. (in fact, Paul takes great care to list some of them in 1 Corinthians 15), and we read in Acts 1 that the person chosen to replace Judas had to have been an eyewitness.

The beginning of 1 John is one of the most lucid descriptions of what participant/eyewitness testimony involves: *"That which was from the beginning, which we have **heard**, which we have **seen with our eyes**, which we have **looked at** and our hands have **touched**—this we proclaim concerning the Word of life. The life appeared; we have _seen it_ and testify to it, and we proclaim to you the eternal life, which was with the Father and has **appeared to us**. We proclaim to you what we have **seen** and **heard**, so that you also may have fellowship with us. And our fellowship is with the Father and with his Son, Jesus Christ. We write this to make our joy complete."* [63]

God calls us to experience him, for example, He says *"Taste and see that the LORD is good"* [64]. He says that when we follow him, our experience of Him will be relational and experiential, not intellectual. He says, *"Here I am! I stand at the door and knock. If anyone hears my voice and opens the door, I will come in and eat with that person, and they with me"*[65] .

Each one of us needs to have a personal encounter with a risen Lord before we can effectively communicate Him to others.

Witness is Invitation, not Confrontation.

Andrew goes to Peter and brings him to Jesus. Witness is not confrontation, it is invitation! This also happens elsewhere in the Gospel accounts where people are brought to Jesus, so for example we read of a Samaritan Woman in John 4: *"Then, leaving her water jar, the woman went back to the town and said to the people, "Come, see a man who told me everything I ever did. Could this be the Christ?" They came out of the town and made their way toward him."*

We live in a confrontational society, almost everything it seems is based on confrontation of some kind. Certainly, the Western electoral and legal systems are predicated on conflict and confrontation, and results being determined by winners and losers, the winners with the most votes, and the losers with the fewest (in an election this happens at the ballot box, in a trial, voting happens behind closed doors in a jury deliberation). The powerful overcome the weak. Lip service is given to truth and what's best, but ultimately the one who wins is the one who is stronger or better or most popular, not the one who is right.

The gospel stands counter to that, proclaiming the gospel is not about winning an argument, it's about introducing people to a saviour! Perhaps we would be more successful if, rather than arguing with people, we tried talking about our experiences with Jesus and inviting others to come and meet with Him.

People will not go to church just because it is there. Posters in shop windows are not enough to fill the church at an evangelistic service, we need to personally invite people to meet with Jesus, but we don't have to convert them. That's God's job.

So, just two thoughts from the disciple Andrew for us to chew over:

1. Let's meet with Jesus for ourselves, and
2. Based on that, invite others to meet with Him for themselves, then perhaps people might say to us what the townsfolk of the Samaritan town said to the woman at the well ... *"We no longer believe just because of what you said; now we have heard for ourselves, and we know that this man really is the Saviour of the world"*[66].

So what?

What is God saying to each one of us?

Firstly, I believe that we all need to hear that even if we think we're invisible, we are not invisible to God. That He can see, and He knows everything we do for Him. We do not have to find a place of prominence before God will use us. We can be faithful to Him even in the obscure place, even in the shadows, and we can know that even the stuff we feel isn't noticed, the things which aren't seen by men, those things ARE seen and noticed by your Father in heaven!

Secondly, you don't have to learn every minute detail and argument of doctrine. Just do what Andrew did, just do what the woman at the well in the Samaritan village did. Invite people to meet with Jesus, stand back and let Him speak peace into their souls. In fact, if you try to do too much, you end up getting in the way. And no one wants to do that!

Occasionally you might hear of someone coming to faith at an evangelistic event, and I would like to tell you about Wendy, my wife, just to illustrate this point.

When my wife Wendy was in her late teens, she was not a Christian. She had no intention of going anywhere near a church. In our city there was a Billy Graham rally, but as she'd never even heard of Billy Graham, the posters meant nothing to her. In fact, she says that at the time she thought he was a candidate in some kind of local election and took no notice.

Wendy, however, loved singing, and her aunt invited her to come to an event and be part of the choir. After all, she could sing and read music and it would be so helpful to have another voice singing.

"I can't come on that day" Wendy told her aunt.

"OK, how about Thursday?"

"Yes, I can make that"

"Good, we'll pick you up, and you can come along with us"

At the event, in a choir of hundreds, looking out at many thousands of people, she realised that she probably wasn't needed in the choir!

Billy Graham spoke powerfully that night and Wendy recalls that even though she was behind him, it was as though he was turning round and looking her in the eye saying "YOU need to get right with God!"

Wendy committed her life to God that night, and the rest, as they say, is history.

She later found out that her aunt hadn't intended to go back to the rally again and that she had cancelled arrangements with other people to take her.

Who is responsible for Wendy coming to faith? God obviously. But in human terms, was it Billy Graham, who preached the message? Or her Aunt who took her there? Clearly, it was Billy Graham's powerful message which Wendy heard and responded to, but would Wendy have even heard it without the involvement of her aunt? Doubtful.

Listen to testimonies about how God has moved, about how people have come to faith. Overwhelmingly, people will tell stories about friends, family members, work colleagues and so on who have impacted them.

The Bible says: *"I sent you to reap what you have not worked for. Others have done the hard work, and you have reaped the benefits of their labour."* [67]

I pray that will be our experience! So that as fellow workers in the harvest, we will both sow for others and reap what others have sown.

3. James (Boanerges)

When you get down to it, doing a study on a Biblical character is not easy. Unlike the vast array of commentaries of the Bible which are available to us, there are few books on characters in the Bible. In addition, for James, there is very little Biblical reference. There are only 17 Bible references to James, and when you look them up and categorise them, you see that they refer to only 8 separate events, so the information we have about him is surprisingly sparse. Having said that, I believe there are things we can learn from what we know about James.

The Bible Texts…

- Matthew 10.2; Mark 3.17; Acts 1.13 James is listed as one of the twelve disciples. We can also note from these references that as part of his listing as an apostle, Christ named him Boanerges (which means "son of thunder").
- Matthew 4.21,22; Mark 1.19,20 and Luke 5.10 record the calling of James.
  Luke 9.52-54 James asks if he should call down fire from heaven.
- Matthew 20.20-21; Mark 10.35-40 James asks for status in the kingdom (His mother on his behalf in the Matthew reference).

- James as one of Christ's "inner circle" of three disciples who are sometimes present when the others aren't, for example:
  - at Jairus' house (Mark 5.37; Luke 8.51);
  - on the mount of Transfiguration (Matthew 17.1-3; Mark 9.2; Luke 9.28);
  - withdrawing with Christ at Gethsemane (Matthew 26.36-37; Mark 14.32-34).
  - Acts 12.1-3 The account of James' death.

Basic information about James.....

James is the English form of the Hebrew name Jacob, which interestingly means "he deceives".

James was a fisherman. He lived and worked on the shores of Galilee with his father and brother (very much like Simon and Andrew). As a fisherman, he would have been a rough character (I imagine he would be like the rough old Cornish fishermen that are portrayed in pictures). Weathered and rough, coarse in their language, inclined to call a spade a spade, and usually very philosophical about life (and death).

James is always described or placed alongside his brother, John. Even in the account of his death, he is described as "James the brother of John". This is probably partly due to the writers' decisions to identify him since there was another disciple called James, and one of Jesus' brothers was also called James, but it is still interesting that his identification is as a brother, rather than as

James the fisherman, or a description of some other aspect of his life or character.

James and his brother John are sons of Zebedee. There are a few hints that the family was relatively wealthy. Firstly, we note that there were "hired hands" that James and John left with their father when they went to follow Jesus. Secondly, we know that John was able to contrive for Peter to be allowed into the high priest's courtyard[68], so it is possible that Zebedee and his family had some standing in the community.

What about James can we draw on?

His Temper

One of the most striking characteristics of James (and his brother John) is his nickname. We read in Mark 3:17 that in the list of the names of the apostles is *"James son of Zebedee and his brother John (to them he gave the name Boanerges, which means "sons of thunder")"*. It is generally accepted that this is because James and John were both hot-tempered men. I want for a few minutes to consider what James teaches us about getting angry and losing our tempers.

I want to start by considering whether there is anything WE are permitted to get angry about. I have read lots of articles about "righteous anger", which say that we CAN, in fact, get angry about something as long as it is "righteous anger".

The argument goes something like this:

1. God is good all the time. He CANNOT do anything "bad" or "wrong".
2. God gets angry.
3. Therefore, since God cannot do anything bad, and He gets angry, there is clearly a form of anger which is "Godly" and therefore not sinful.
4. If we can identify those things which God gets angry about, then we also have the right to be angry about those things because our anger will by definition be "Godly".

   AND that when we get angry about the things God is angry about, our anger is not sinful but "righteous".
5. So, the argument concludes, as long as our anger is 'righteous' (that is, the same anger as God would have), then it is perfectly acceptable.

In fact, some would argue, if we are truly a righteous people then such anger is not only OK, but it is actually REQUIRED of us.

In Luke 9 we read an occasion where James and his brother get angry:_"but the people there did not welcome him because he was heading for Jerusalem. When the disciples James and John saw this, they asked, "Lord, do you want us to call fire down from heaven to destroy them?" But Jesus turned and rebuked them, and they went to another village"_ [69].

Note that using the thought process I outlined above, it could be argued that the anger James and his brother expressed here was righteous, that his outburst was justified and possibly even required. However, this is not what Luke records as Christ's assessment. We read that James and John are rebuked for their anger. James losing his temper with an angry outburst results in a rebuke from Christ. Doesn't sound like it's a good thing after all, does it?

So, I want us to stop, to pause, to consider just a few thoughts ...

1. Does God really need our help to judge what to get angry about?
2. If God is angry about something, is it really necessary for us to be? Are we so arrogant as to believe that our anger somehow adds weight or authenticity to God's?
3. Doesn't God's question in Jonah 4 bring something to the table about whether WE have the right to be angry about anything? *"Is it right for you to be angry?*[70]*"* The subsequent discourse between God and Jonah shows us that no, it isn't.

James 1:20 says, *"for Man's anger does not bring about the righteous life that God desires"*. So, what does man's anger bring? What does anger do? Here are a few things the Bible says:

1. In the sermon on the mount, Jesus talks about anger, he says, *"You have heard that it was said to the people long ago, 'You shall not murder, and anyone who murders will be subject to judgment.' But I tell you that anyone who is angry with a brother or sister will be subject to judgment[71]."* Jesus puts anger in the same category as murder, and he doesn't qualify it by saying "if anyone is angry without reason", or "this doesn't apply if your anger is righteous." He simply says, "anyone who is angry". Anger makes us subject to judgment.

2. Psalm 37:8 says:_*"Refrain from anger, and forsake wrath! Fret not yourself; it tends only to evil"*. And Ephesians 4:26-27 says: _*"In your anger do not sin; do not let the sun go down on your anger, and do not give the devil a foothold"*. Anger inclines us to evil and gives Satan a place in our lives.

3. Ecclesiastes 7:9 exhorts us not to be _*"quick in your spirit to become angry, for anger lodges in the bosom of fools"*, and Proverbs 29:11 says,_*"A fool gives full vent to his spirit, but a wise man quietly holds it back"*. Anger reveals our foolishness.

4. Proverbs 22:24 says of anger, _*"Make no friendship with a man given to anger, nor go with a wrathful man"*, and Proverbs 15:18 says, _*"A hot-tempered man stirs up strife, but he who is slow to anger quiets contention"*. Anger fuels conflict and inhibits friendship.

I read this quote recently and thought it applies really well to our thoughts on this subject: 'Anger is a wind that blows out the lamp of the mind'. It is not without reason that we have to be reminded not to sin when we are angry. Anger often has the effect of triggering actions and words which are out of character, of blinding us to the consequences of our words and actions. It leads us to do things which we just wouldn't do if we weren't angry. For many, there is a tendency to allow the emotions to rule the mind, which give rise to poorly thought out responses, especially if you're like me and prone to making on the spot reactions and decisions, we should learn from this. Let's not allow our anger to cloud our judgment.

Jesus says it is not just the action that God judges, it is the inner man, the thought life. So for example, in the sermon on the mount, Jesus roots his teaching in the importance of what happens in the heart and the mind and the Spirit.

We've already noted that he says about anger, he says the same about lust:_"anyone who LOOKS at a woman lustfully has already committed adultery with her IN HIS HEART"_[72]. Jesus expects a new standard of us.

I believe that the right way of approaching our anger is by:

1. Submission to Christ. With repentance where necessary.
2. Daily picking up your cross and following Christ.

3. Allowing the Holy Spirit to work in you and through you.

And this is true for all our emotions, not just anger!

His Ambition for Status

James seemed to always be right at the heart of the discussions about who would be the greatest. On one occasion, His mother asked Jesus if James and his brother John could sit either side of Him. The desire for position and influence is a powerful one. Running through society, and sadly the church, is a seam of this desire to be first. We jostle and struggle with each other about who is better than whom, who will be the greatest, who has more status.

This is very pertinent at the moment. Whilst I was writing this chapter, I watched the transition of power in the USA from Donald Trump to Joe Biden, and whatever you think of the result of the election, whether you feel it is good or bad for the USA and the World, one thing that all politicians seem to have in common is that they all see themselves as "servants" of the people. This has got me thinking because when I look at most of the leaders on the world stage of whatever political persuasion, I don't see much evidence of real servanthood.

Even in the church, there are not many who call themselves leaders who are truly servants. We tend to run straight to the lists in Titus and Timothy to measure a leader's suitability, yet let's start with Jesus.

Jesus is unconcerned with stuff like ability to plan, or cast vision or organise people. He says things like this.

- *"Anyone who wants to be first must be the very last, and the servant of all"*[73].
- *"Whoever wants to become great among you must be your servant, and whoever wants to be first must be your slave"*[74].
- *"The greatest among you should be like the youngest, and the one who rules like the one who serves"*[75].

In a nutshell, Jesus says if you want to be first, you must become the servant of all. We all serve something. The question we must all answer is this … "What/who do we serve?"

I believe the strong teaching and witness of the Bible is this … if you are not prepared to serve, and I don't mean by just playing with words and re-classifying your role as that of a servant. I mean ACTUALLY menially serving (wash up, push a broom, clean toilets, put out chairs, do car park duty), then you have NO BUSINESS aspiring to leadership in the church, or anywhere else for that matter. I believe one of the critical measures of your suitability as a leader should be in your attitude towards serving.

Jesus himself said, *"the last will be first, and the first will be last."* His teaching on who will be the greatest shows that we should not look for status on this earth, we should look to be servants of each other. Otherwise, we fall into the "James trap" of selfishness and seeking status.

Commitment

There are numerous references in the Bible about commitment in various aspects of life: to our families, neighbours, employers, the church, our health, and in all things we do and say[76]. But the Bible teaches that our **primary** commitment should be to God Himself. Jesus said, *"You shall love the Lord your God with **all** your heart and with **all** your soul and with **all** your mind. This is the great and first commandment"* [77].

Jesus is telling us that every fibre of our being, every part of our lives, must be committed to loving and serving God. This means that we must hold nothing back from Him because God holds nothing back from us, so we can read verses like these and know the extent of his love for us:

- John 3:16 *"For God so loved the world that he gave his one and only Son, that whoever believes in him shall not perish but have eternal life."*
- Romans 8:32 *"He who did not spare his own Son, but gave him up for us all—how will he not also, along with him, graciously give us all things?"*

Paul can burst into praise and pray this for the Ephesians: *"I pray that out of his glorious riches he may strengthen you with power through his Spirit in your inner being, so that Christ may dwell in your hearts through faith. And I pray that you, being rooted and established in love, may have power, together with all the Lord's holy people, to grasp how wide and long and high and deep is the love of Christ, and to know this love that surpasses knowledge—that you may be filled to the measure of all the fullness of God.*

Now to him who is able to do immeasurably more than all we ask or imagine, according to his power that is at work within us, to him be glory in the church and in Christ Jesus through-out all generations, for ever and ever! Amen"[78]. If God's love for us is so great and so extensive, what should our response be?

Jesus tells us that our commitment to Him must even trump our commitment to our families: *"If anyone comes to Me and does not hate* [79] *his own father and mother and wife and children and brothers and sisters, yes, and even his own life, he cannot be My disciple. Whoever does not bear his own cross and come after Me cannot be my disciple"* [80]. Such commitment means that although our family relationships are important, our commitment to Christ demands that if we are given an 'us or him' ultimatum, we turn away from them and continue on with Jesus[81]. There are people all over the world now in the 21st century who have to make that very choice, and as our faith increasingly becomes unfashionable and abhorrent to the 'civilised' west, we may have to as well. The bottom line is that those who cannot make that kind of commitment cannot be His disciple.

Revelation 12:11 is a favourite of many people, it says, *"they* (the saints) *overcame him* (the devil) *by the blood of the lamb and the word of their testimony"* and what Christian wouldn't want that? But Revelation 12:11 says more than that. The second half of the verse goes on to say this: *"they did not love their lives so much as to shrink from death"*. That's not so encouraging, is it? The prospect of suffering and even the ultimate sacrifice of martyrdom are part of the package for Christians. Jesus says things like *"if they persecuted me, they will persecute you also"*[82], and *"I have told you these things, so that in me you may have peace. In this world you will have trouble …"*[83].

That is the bad news, the good news is that the Bible commends and speaks incredibly highly of faithful believers who pay the ultimate price for their witness. John saw in his vision of the millennium those martyred for their faith reigning with Christ for a thousand years[84]. Peter, who wrote a great deal about martyrdom and suffering for one's faith, said, *"If you are insulted because of the name of Christ, you are blessed, for the Spirit of glory and of God rests on you... However, if you suffer as a Christian, do not be ashamed, but praise God that you bear that name"* [85]. Jesus pronounces a blessing upon those who are persecuted for His name: *"Blessed are you when people insult you, persecute you and falsely say all kinds of evil against you because of me"* [86].

Although we do have accounts of some early martyrs in the Bible, Stephen in Acts 6 for example, and although except for John, ALL the disciples were martyred for their faith, James is the only disciple whose martyrdom is actually recorded in Scripture. So in one way he really was the first among the disciples — Be careful what you ask God for!!

We cannot say that James' commitment to Christ was half-hearted. For all of his faults, James was prepared to pay the price for his faith. A quick temper, an elevated sense of self-importance did not block his wholehearted commitment to the Lord. Let us learn that wholehearted commitment is what God requires of us, and is nothing less than He deserves.

James is an example for us to follow. Jesus calls us to commitment, not just to lip service. D.C. Talk is a Christian band, and in their Album "Jesus Freak" there is a recording of someone saying the following statement: "the biggest cause of atheism in our country today are Christians themselves. That Christians can go to a church on a Sunday morning, worship him with their lips and then deny him with their lifestyle, that is what an unbelieving world simply finds unbelievable[87]". Will we do that? Will we just pay "lip service" to Christ and not follow through with our actions and our lifestyles? In other words, will our commitment have substance? Have we counted the cost?

"When I survey the Wondrous Cross", concludes with these words :

"Were the whole realm of nature mine
That were an offering far too small

Love so amazing, so divine
Demands my soul my life my all[88]"

James' example is an unhesitating response to Jesus' call on his life. Will we likewise without hesitation follow the Lord's call on our lives?

Conclusions

Finally, I find James really encouraging, especially after considering the failings that he had in the area of his self-control and his desires for status that we read about.

Despite his failings, James was selected by our Lord as part of what might be described as an "inner circle": the multitudes, the 72, the 12 and the 3 [89]. Despite his failings, James was party to a particularly close relationship with the Lord..

This is really encouraging!

God desires relationship with us despite what we're like, despite how much we fail, despite how much we become like those around us and try to climb up the ladder in the church so to speak, there is always a place for close fellowship with Christ.

My prayer for you is that you really understand and make part of you the absolute assurance of that great love of God. Having done that, whether the pressure to give up comes from outside, through persecution of some sort, or whether it is within, perhaps in the form of an emotion which keeps getting the better of you, that your faith develops into one which shines out for all to see.

4. John (Boanerges)

John is the author of the Gospel of John, the letters of John and the book of Revelation. Aside from Luke (27%) and Paul (23%), he has written more of the New Testament than any other author (20%). (These three authors between them account for 70% of the New Testament!).

John lived in Galilee, probably in Bethsaida [90]; He was son of Zebedee and brother of James. Comparison of Matthew 27:55,56, Mark 15:40, 41 and John 19:25 suggest that John's mother was called Salome and that she was Mary's sister. If this is true, John and his brother James were cousins of Jesus and he is also related to John the Baptist.

Zebedee's family were fishermen on the Sea of Galilee. It is reasonable to believe that the family had at least some means, as they had hired servants and were therefore employers[91]. If the belief that Salome was his mother is true, it adds weight to this, as she was one of the financial supporters of Jesus[92]. This makes Jesus' words about rich people and the kingdom of Heaven interesting, as John's family is a very real example of a family entering the kingdom which whilst not necessarily rich, would certainly not have been poor!

John was initially a disciple of John the Baptist, he becomes an apostle of Jesus [93]. John has a place in the group of three apostles closest to Jesus (the others are Peter and James), so with the other two, he witnessed first hand some of the events that the other nine disciples did not, for example, when Jesus raised Jairus's daughter[94], the transfiguration[95], and Gethsemane[96]; John asked Jesus to call down fire on Samaritans, and he was given the name Boanerges by Jesus[97]; John and James mother requested that they be given places of special honour in the coming kingdom[98]; John and Peter prepared the Passover[99]; It was John who lay close to Jesus' breast at the Last Supper[100]. He was present at Jesus' trial[101]. He stood at the foot of the cross[102], recognised Jesus at the Sea of Galilee[103]. Active with Peter in the apostolic church[104], and recognised by Paul as one of the pillars of the church[105] who extended their "grace" toward him. Finally, he was exiled to Patmos *"because of the word of God and the testimony of Jesus"*[106] where he wrote the book of Revelation.

My focus here is this: You cannot really think about the disciple John without thinking about the really close relationship he had with Jesus and about how much Jesus loved him. Even to the extent that on the cross, as Jesus own mother was there, a dying Jesus says to Mary, *"here is your son"*, and to John *"here is your mother"*, and we read that from the time on, the disciple took her into his home[107]. Jesus trusted John with his own mother. John knew he was loved by Jesus and his gospel significantly reflects that knowledge as the only description you will find of him in it is *"the disciple Jesus loved"*[108]. He was so touched and transformed by that love that his creed became 'love one another' and his letters exude that.

This is even more significant because John, along with his brother James was named Boanerges by Jesus because of his hot temper! It is significant that the person who wrote a gospel and letters which express a focus and desire to show the world the love of God is actually one of the two most hot-tempered disciples. What a transformation!

He describes himself as "the disciple Jesus loved".

This is a strong statement that John knew his place in Jesus' heart. We live in a time where there is what can only be described as an epidemic of mental health problems, in the church one of the most common pastoral issues I have encountered over the last 30 years has been a very low opinion of who we are.

When I was growing up, one of my most painful memories was people laughing at me. It happened a lot. This even happened at home with family jokes and teasing (although there was no malicious intent). I grew up feeling second rate because it seemed to me that everything I did or tried to do became a subject for teasing. I learned that everything I thought or did was in some way a joke. It took decades for me to overcome the damage that did to my self-image.

You may remember things said to you or about you by parents, siblings, teachers, friends and even strangers. They can range from comments about physical appearance, through intellectual, sporting, artistic or some other lack of ability, to comments about character. Often it seems that everything anyone ever says either to you, or about you, impacts how you see yourself, and in one way that is true. It is not without reason that Paul tells the Ephesians not to let any unwholesome talk to come out of their mouths, but only that which builds others up according to their needs.

> There is one specific thing which can be said to people which I have had to help them to overcome, and it is so devastating to them, I want to just take a moment aside and address it specifically.
>
> Over the years I have had far too many people come across my threshold who have been damaged because they have been told they were a mistake. So, if you have been told you are a mistake, you need to hear this: God does NOT make mistakes. You are not a mistake, you may have been unplanned, but you were known by God in the depths of your mother's womb. He saw every bone being formed, every muscle growing, very electrical neural impulse in your brain as it was developing. He was there every moment of your formation and growth.

We must recapture and reclaim our understanding of

1. **How God sees us**. We must get to the place where we really do understand just how much God values us.
2. **How we see ourselves**. We must get a right self-image before God, thinking of ourselves neither too highly, nor too lowly.
3. **How we see others**. We must understand how much God thinks of other people, and that understanding must impact how we treat them.

The foundation of our self-image lies in our understanding of how God sees us. Put simply, if we can truly grasp how God sees us, it will transform how we view ourselves.

In a nutshell, God says this to you: You have immense value. Here are some of the things he would say to you ...

1. I am the Creator and you are my creation. I breathed into your nostrils the breath of life[109].
2. I created you in my own image[110].
3. My eyes saw your unformed substance[111].
4. I knit you together in your mother's womb[112].
5. You are fearfully and wonderfully made[113].
6. I know the number of hairs on your head, and before a word is on your tongue, I know it[114].
7. You are more valuable than many sparrows[115].

8. I have given you dominion over all sheep and oxen and all beasts of the field and birds of the heavens and fish of the sea[116].
9. I have crowned you with glory and honour as the pinnacle and final act of the six days of creation[117].

He also declares that not only are you valuable to Him, but He loves you ...

1. He loves you so much that He sent His son[118].
2. This is love, not that we loved God, but that he loved us and sent his son as an atoning sacrifice for our sins[119].
3. God demonstrated his own love for us in this: while we were still sinners, Christ died for us[120].

We really must get this in. If we can really grasp this truth and take it into our souls, we will be able to endure all sorts of stuff we otherwise wouldn't.

So, what is a healthy self-image? There are some references which suggest that people have struggled with this for thousands of years ...

- *"O LORD, what is man that you regard him, or the son of man that you think of him? Man is like a breath; his days are like a passing shadow"*[121].
- *"But I am a worm and not a man, scorned by everyone, despised by the people. All who see me mock me; they hurl insults, shaking their heads"*[122].

- "How then can man be in the right before God? How can he who is born of woman be pure? Behold, even the moon is not bright, and the stars are not pure in his eyes; how much less man, who is a maggot, and the son of man, who is a worm"[123].

The Bible describes God using people who had a bad self-image...

Moses didn't think he was suitable to go to Pharaoh (in fact, he asked God to send someone else):

- "But Moses said to God, "Who am I that I should go to Pharaoh and bring the Israelites out of Egypt?"[124].
- "But Moses said, "Pardon your servant, Lord. Please send someone else"[125]

Jeremiah thought he was too young: "Alas, Sovereign LORD," I said, "I do not know how to speak; I am too young"[126].

Gideon didn't think he came from the right family: "Pardon me, my lord," Gideon replied, "but how can I save Israel? My clan is the weakest in Manasseh, and I am the least in my family"[127].

King Saul initially struggled with self-image problems: "Saul answered, "But am I not a Benjamite, from the smallest tribe of Israel, and is not my clan the least of all the clans of the tribe of Benjamin? Why do you say such a thing to me?"[128].

A correct self-image depends on us truly understanding what God thinks of us. We must understand our immense value to God, yet we must also be wary of falling into pride, of getting an over inflated opinion of ourselves.

We read of Uzziah, who we are told that *"after Uzziah became powerful, his pride led to his downfall"* [129]. James 4:6 says, *"God opposes the proud but shows favour to the humble"*. Jesus himself says,_ "For those who exalt themselves will be humbled, and those who humble themselves will be exalted"._ [130]

Our self-image should be rooted not in what we do, but rather in who we are in Christ. We need to humble ourselves before Him, and He will honour us. Psalm 16:2 reminds us, *"I said to the Lord, 'You are my Lord; apart from you, I have no good thing'."* We must understand that our self-worth and esteem comes best by having a right relationship with God. We can know we are valuable because of the high price God paid for us through the blood of His Son, Jesus Christ.

And this impacts on how we look upon other people, and I believe the key to this lies in two sections of Scripture:

1. *"Do nothing out of selfish ambition or vain conceit. Rather, in humility value others above yourselves, not looking to your own interests but each of you to the interests of the others. In your relationships with one another, have the same mindset as Christ Jesus".* [131]

2. And_ "For by the grace given me I say to every one of you: Do not think of yourself more highly than you ought, but rather think of yourself with sober judgment, in accordance with the faith God has distributed to each of you."_[132]

Note, here, the ingredients of proper self-image:

1. Removing bad and wrong motivations
2. Recognising the value of the people around us

John changes from "Boanerges" to the disciple of love.

John changes from someone with a really hot temper to one who writes a Gospel, 3 letters and Revelation and the theme of his book is very much focused on love.

John "the disciple Jesus loved", whose creed was "love one another" and whose letters exude this desire that we show the world the love of God is actually one of the two disciples Jesus named "boanerges", a son of thunder!

What a transformation — from a hot-tempered "son of thunder" to the "disciple Jesus loved", from the disciple who wanted to call down fire from heaven to destroy towns for their sinfulness, to one who could so eloquently describe the love of God like this ...

1. *"For God so loved the world that her gave his only son, Jesus Christ, that whoever believes in him shall not perish, but have eternal life"*[133].
2. *"This is love, not that we loved God, but that He loved us and sent his son as an atoning sacrifice for our sins"*[134].

From the disciple who argued with his brother and the other disciples about who was going to be the greatest and sit in the place of honour at Jesus' right hand, to the one who remembers and records Jesus command to put one another first and prefer their needs to your own.

John's transformation is astounding!

When we meet with Jesus, we can be completely changed. Paul often writes that once we were something, but now in Christ we are something different, so for example, he says to the Ephesians *"For you were once darkness, but now you are light in the Lord"*[135]. In 1 Corinthians he gives a great long description of what it looks like to be outside the kingdom of God, and he says, *"that is what some of you were"* [136]. And in 2 Corinthians he says: *"Therefore, if anyone is in Christ, the new creation has come: The old has gone, the new is here!*[137].

This is GOOD news!, and I'll tell you why …

Many people live under a cloud of belief that they cannot change. They might have a habit they just can't seem to get the better of. Perhaps like the Apostle John, they have a temper and seem to be consistently in conflict, lurching from one fight to another. They may be a slave to something they can't get the better of. Drinking, or smoking or drugs, or even chocolate. It might be a relationship; people lurch from one toxic relationship to another, always choosing the bad ones. All sorts of things have the potential to enslave you.

The good news John teaches us is this: There is hope for our future. Our past does not define our future, our habits do not control our eternity, our character flaws can be turned around by the grace of God. New life in Jesus Christ means exactly that, he transforms our nature and gives us a hope and a future. Now that's GOOD news! We can learn from this that something even quite deeply ingrained in us need not direct and drive us.

Jesus trusts John with his mother.

"Near the cross of Jesus stood his mother, his mother's sister, Mary the wife of Clopas, and Mary Magdalene. When Jesus saw his mother there, and the disciple whom he loved standing nearby, he said to her, "Woman, here is your son," and to the disciple, "Here is your mother." From that time on, this disciple took her into his home"[138].

Wow!

Jesus trusted John with his own mother. What, or who, does God trust you with? How are you handling it/them?

I think the Bible passage which springs immediately to mind is the parable which Jesus told about three servants, and about how they handled the money the master left them in charge of when he went away. God calls us to invest the resources He makes available to us. God gives us all sorts of resources and talents, and if we do nothing with them, our ability to respond and be useful will diminish to vanishing point. This is a warning against laziness, fear of change or unwillingness to take risks. If we lie in bed and do nothing, atrophy takes over, and we find we do less and less. We lose even the muscles we once had. It is like that in the spiritual realm. Those who neglect or squander what is given risk losing even what they have, but those who show their faithfulness by working, by using what God has entrusted them with can be sure that they will receive a great reward!

I often shy away from this kind of emphasis because in it there is a risk that we will fall into the trap of believing that it is what we DO that is important to God, we risk elevating works above faith. But there are some passages among which is this one, which do show us that although we are saved by faith, not works, what we do in this life does have eternal implications …

So, for example, we have a passage in Corinthians which says:

"But each one should build with care. For no one can lay any foundation other than the one already laid, which is Jesus Christ. If anyone builds on this foundation using gold, silver, costly stones, wood, hay or straw, their work will be shown for

what it is, because the Day will bring it to light. It will be revealed with fire, and the fire will test the quality of each person's work. If what has been built survives, the builder will receive a reward. If it is burned up, the builder will suffer loss, but yet will be saved—even though only as one escaping through the flames"[139].

In Revelation, we also read:

- "Then all the churches will know that I am he who searches hearts and minds, and I will repay each of you according to your deeds"[140];
- "Another book was opened, which is the book of life. The dead were judged according to what they had done as recorded in the books"[141];
- "Look, I am coming soon! My reward is with me, and I will give to each person according to what they have done"[142].

We will be both judged and rewarded according to what we have done. Jesus also says in Matthew 7:16ff, "By their fruit you will recognise them. Do people pick grapes from thorn bushes, or figs from thistles? Likewise, every good tree bears good fruit, but a bad tree bears bad fruit. A good tree cannot bear bad fruit, and a bad tree cannot bear good fruit. Every tree that does not bear good fruit is cut down and thrown into the fire. Thus, by their fruit you will recognise them".

The bottom line, then, is that we are called to be stewards of the things God has entrusted to us, and how we manage those resources may well have eternal implications.

There are two things that I believe we must really get to grips with when it comes to caring for and managing what God has given us.

The **main thing** that God is trusting us with is the gospel itself.

Do you think that if He wanted to, God couldn't think of or find another mechanism for telling the world about the Gospel?

But he hasn't!

We talk a lot about us choosing God, but God chose US. John 15:16 says, *You did not choose me, but I chose you and appointed you so that you might go and bear fruit — fruit that will last — and so that whatever you ask in my name the Father will give you.*

The **second thing** God gives us and trusts us with are people.

This is shown in this particular exchange with Jesus, but we can read all sorts of Bible verses and passages which show the very high-value God places on people and on how we look after them.

Psalm 127 says children are a gift from the Lord [143]

We read in more than one place that God's heart is for the orphan and the widow, both of whom are types of people without families"

-   Psalm 68:6 says, *"God sets the lonely in families"*.

- James 1:27 says, *"Religion that God our Father accepts as pure and faultless is this: to look after orphans and widows in their distress"*.
- Deuteronomy 14:28-29 instructs the Israelites: *"At the end of every three years, bring all the tithes of that year's produce and store it in your towns, so that the Levites (who have no allotment or inheritance of their own) and the foreigners,* **the fatherless and the widows** *who live in your towns may come and eat and be satisfied, and so that the LORD your God may bless you in all the work of your hands"*.
- Job 31:16-18 describes Job defending his righteousness and in it, he says that from his youth he *"reared the fatherless as a father would,* and *guided the widow, providing for them, defending them"*.
- Psalms 146:9 says, *"The LORD watches over the foreigner and sustains the fatherless and the widow, but he frustrates the ways of the wicked"*.;
- Isaiah 1:17 says, *"Learn to do right; seek justice. Defend the oppressed. Take up the cause of the fatherless; plead the case of the widow"*.

On a broader note, I believe that we are all gifts from God to one another. When we start to see others like that, we are and will be much more inclined to treat them with love and compassion and grace. No human on this planet is ultimately your enemy.

The Bible says we don't fight against flesh and blood, but against rulers and authorities and the forces of this dark world[144].

I think I'm going to leave you with this thought: After Jesus said to John *this is your mother*, we read that *From that time on, this disciple took her into his home*[145]. In other words, he didn't go home and pray about it, he didn't spend days thinking about it. He acted on what God said. There and then.

The very next person you look at, ask God to really show you how much He loves and values that person, and how He would have you relate to them so that they really can see God's care of and love for them through you. It might be a member of your natural family, a spouse, sibling, child, parent, or it might be someone you are not naturally related to. My challenge to you is to follow through on that and actually relate to them. Not tomorrow or next week sometime, but from this moment on ...

History records that John did not leave Jerusalem or start any ministry journeys until after Mary had died. He stayed with her and loved and cared for her for the rest of her natural life. This challenge is not for the next week or the next month, but for the long term, for the rest of your life.

5. Philip

The first three gospels virtually ignore Philip, he is included in their lists of the disciples, but that is all. Only John gives us more detail.

> *There is mention of a believer called Philip in Acts. He appears in Acts 8 where he preaches the word in Samaria, he also meets with the Ethiopian Eunuch and baptises him, then gets miraculously transported by the Spirit to another area and then at the end of Acts, (20 years later) he is recorded as giving hospitality to Paul and his companions. For various reasons, it is generally understood this is not the disciple Philip, but is more likely to be the Philip listed as one of the first deacons chosen in Acts 6. This is not the place to explain those reasons, but I accept this interpretation, so if you wonder why I'm not mentioning the Philip we read about in Acts, that is why — he's a different Philip!*

Accepting that understanding, the only real detail about Philip comes from John's gospel, which records 4 interactions Philip has with Jesus ...

1. John 1:43-46. Philip goes to Nathaniel and brings him to Jesus.
2. John 6:5. Jesus tests Philip about food for the 5,000

3. John 12:21f. Philip brings some Greeks to Andrew who want to meet Jesus, and they both go to Jesus.
4. John 14:8-11. Philip says to Jesus, *"show us the Father and that will be enough for us"*.

So, what do these actions teach us?

Friendship

Philip is a name which is derived from the Greek word Phileo, which means friend. It has often been said that people's names are significant, and noted how regularly we live up to our names.

Philip was such a person, the first thing he did when he met Jesus was go to his friend Nathanael.

Friendship is important. It is one of the most important sources of influence in our lives. It is particularly visible in children, but it is just as important in adulthood. Memes about real friendship abound on social media, but if you boil them down, they all suggest that a friend, a true friend, is the one who sticks with you through thick and thin, the one who will not only share the high spots of your life, but who will also stick with you through the low spots, who will overlook your irritating habits and who will quickly forgive you in times of conflict.

I want to camp out on what friendship is, and how important it is for a few moments.

There is an old saying which says: "Choose your friends wisely. Because you will become what they are", the Romans used to say "if you lie down with dogs, you get up with fleas", and in Corinthians Paul quotes another proverb of the day saying "bad company corrupts good character". Friendship is important.

However, there does appear to be a dichotomy or ambivalence about friends in the Bible. On the one hand, we are called to be like Christ, who seemed to go out of his way to befriend all sorts of undesirable people. As Christians, we believe that we should proclaim the gospel to all the world, and act to overcome any political, social, geographical or ethnic (or any other) boundaries which might come between us and people. In fact, the parable of the dishonest servant seems to be an instruction to us our resources on this earth to get friends. When Jesus says: *"I tell you, use worldly wealth to gain friends for yourselves, so that when it is gone, you will be welcomed into eternal dwellings"* [146]. It seems clear that Jesus is talking about gaining friends who will enter the kingdom with us. We even have a term for it — 'Friendship Evangelism'. The idea being to build friendships with people and on the foundation of that friendship, we share our faith. Someone once described it as 'building a bridge strong enough for the Gospel to cross on'. And studies over decades have shown that by far and away the most successful form of evangelism is through our friendship with people.

On the other hand, we are told not to be friends with the world. James 4:4 says, *"don't you know that*

friendship with the world means enmity against God? There-
fore, anyone who chooses to be a friend of the world becomes
an enemy of God", and I've already quoted Paul's statement in Corinthians about bad company corrupting
character. Jesus himself said people will hate us because
of our faith in him [147].

So, how do we reconcile the apparent desire of our
Lord that we build friendships, with the teaching not to
cultivate wrong friendships? Maybe the example of Jesus will show us this ...

1. Jesus called his disciples his friends [148], yet Luke
   records that he spent the night praying to God before naming them [149].
   - Shows he took great care about who he chose to
     be his friends.
   - Shows a reliance on God's guidance about who
     he chose as friends.
2. Jesus clearly had "circles" of friends. Some were
   basically a crowd who followed Him and we might
   struggle with giving them the label "friend", others
   were in a large group (the 72), then there was a
   smaller group (the 12), then an intimate few (the 3).
   He clearly gave some people more access to him, in
   terms of physical presence, time, depth of teaching
   (including revealing things about himself) than he
   did to others. Be careful about what you reveal to
   whom.
3. Jesus never allowed his friends to stop him from
   truth telling. He was sometimes quite blunt with his

friends. On one occasion, he calls them stupid[150]. In John's gospel, he allows people to leave him (and asks the disciples if they will leave him too), in fact, he doesn't stop Judas leaving when he is revealed as the traitor. Famously, he even calls Peter Satan! His friendship with the disciples was never allowed to interfere with his relationship with God.

For us, the implications are fairly obvious: choose our friends carefully, don't spread them too thin, but invest in a few, and never, ever allow a friend to interfere with your faith. If a friend does that, I would say they are not a true friend. Remember, Paul says, *"Do not be yoked together with unbelievers. For what do righteousness and wickedness have in common?"*[151]. This verse is often quoted in the context of marriage, but it is not Paul's focus. He is talking about all human relationships, including friendships.

The next thing which I want to bring out of this is the concept of being a friend of God, which, unsurprisingly, comes from the Bible.

In the book of James we read *"And the scripture was fulfilled that says, "Abraham believed God, and it was credited to him as righteousness," and he was called God's friend"*[152]. The writer of 2 Chronicles describes Abraham as God's friend, *"Our God, did you not drive out the inhabitants of this land before your people Israel and give it forever to the descendants of Abraham your friend?"*[153], as does

Isaiah *"But you, Israel, my servant, Jacob, whom I have chosen, you descendants of Abraham my friend"*[154].

Jesus says to the disciples *"I call you my friends"* in John 15, and he specifies what a friend of God does, how a friend of God acts: *"if you do what I command"* [155].

So, friendship with God is possible, in fact, we should pursue it. God is not just some divine dictator barking orders or directions from heaven, waiting for us to muck up, so he can smite us. If you live with that kind of image of God, then I'm not surprised if you don't want to follow him.

No, Jesus came and lived among us so that we could shake off that kind of understanding of God, and give us a way to the place where we can say for ourselves, "God is my friend".

And going back to the saying I quoted earlier "choose your friends wisely, because you will become what they are", when we make a point of protecting and developing our friendship with God, actually living and acting in a Godly way becomes less of an effort - we will naturally grow to be like him. In other words, if you want to become more Godly, choose to live your life with him as your friend!

Witness

Philip was From Bethsaida, he led his friend Nathanael to Jesus[156]. Jesus first called Philip personally, and Philip trusted and followed him.

Bringing people to Jesus can seem a very daunting prospect. So many things seem like massive barriers to us. Philip's example shows us that telling people about Jesus need not be like that. All we have to do is tell our friends, take them to Jesus, then withdraw and leave them to him. This is actually really easy.

Firstly, Philip says to his friend, *"we have found the one about whom the Moses wrote"*[157]. He knows that this is something which would spark Nathanael's interest. It is often said that we should only scratch where people are itching! Don't answer questions for people they are not asking, all that does is antagonise them.

Secondly, when Nathanael questions Jesus's origin by saying, *"Nazareth? Can anything good come from there?"*[158] Philip's response is not to try to argue or justify, he merely says, *"come and see"*. He uses the same words that Jesus used on more than one occasion "come and see" (in fact the invitation "come" is the great invitation of the grace of God.) We don't need to intellectually prove Jesus' existence, all we need to do is make the offer, "come and see for yourself". Jesus can touch people's hearts without fancy arguments from us.

When he was confronted with more doubt, Philip also used the Scriptures. His evidence was Moses and the prophets. It is good to tie in our witness to the word of God.

What we can learn from this story is that our role is to point the way, not to convince or pressurise people, and we have a great resource in the Scriptures to draw on in our witness.

Our aim should simply be to introduce people to Jesus, to encourage them to meet with Him, rather than trying to argue them into becoming Christians (which is so often the case).

Philip's first thought was to go to someone he knew well. I touched on this above when I talked about Philip being a friend, but too often when we think about evangelism, we think in terms of going to total strangers. Sometimes it even involves learning a new language and moving to a new country, but Philip teaches us that every one of us has a rich seam of gold right in front of our noses. Friends, neighbours, family members, work colleagues, people who are members of the clubs we are in, we meet all sorts of people in all sorts of ways, and every one needs to know the peace of God, yet so often we neglect it. Sometimes it is embarrassment, sometimes it is fear of being ridiculed or rejected, sometimes we have blotted our copybook by the way we have acted. Witnessing to someone who knows you warts and all can force you to look very closely at how (or if) your actions really do match your claims of faith, and that can be a very uncomfortable place to be.

Finally, the first attempt to witness was actually rebuffed. Nathanael questioned Philip's testimony about Jesus[159]. We should note that Philip didn't try to address the question, he didn't argue with Nathanael, as we've noted, he invited him to "come and see". He changed tack, and it worked. If at first you don't succeed, then give up? NO — try again. Do not be discouraged by someone's apparent rejection of the Gospel.

Perhaps another approach will work better. We would do well if we did that. We don't have to argue Jesus' corner. Having introduced Jesus to people, all we need to do is leave him to it!

So, here are some 'take homes' from Philip's way of bringing people to Jesus that we can learn from..

1. Philip witnessed to his friend Nathanael - we don't have to present the gospel to total strangers to be effective witnesses.
2. Philip introduced Jesus in terms that Nathanael was already familiar with. Look for and find points of connection for people.
3. When Nathanael responded negatively, Philip didn't argue or give up, he changed tack.
4. Philip introduced Nathanael to Jesus and then left him to it. Successful evangelism is not measured in conversions. It is measured in introductions.

Testing

The third thing I want to think about comes from the account of the feeding of the 5,000. In John's description of this event in John 6[160], we read that Jesus asked Philip a question. When all the crowds are all around him, Jesus asks Philip, *"where shall we buy bread for people to eat?"* One thing that really strikes me is that John explains WHY Jesus asks Philip the question: *"He asked this*

*only to **test him**, for he already had in mind what he was go-*
ing to do."

Philip's response to Jesus' test was to ask how they could raise enough to buy food then, having counted the cost, he concludes that they would need 8 months' wages and even then it would not be enough. Too often we think money is the answer to all of our problems, that if we throw money at it, the problem will go away. In Christ, such considerations fall short of His will. I sometimes ponder, did Philip pass the test with this answer?

Does God do or say things, or conversely NOT do or say anything, but leave us in the dark sometimes to test us?

I hated tests when I was growing up. It seemed to me that everything I did was measured in a test. At school, in scouts, at Sunday school, everything we learnt was subject to testing, and I never saw the point. When I was 18, I sat in my mum's car and a man sat in the seat beside me. He had a clipboard, and I had to drive where he told me to drive, I had to complete the manoeuvres he asked me to complete, and I had to answer the questions he asked me about the Highway Code and the car, and its maintenance. I'm talking about my driving test, of course. Passing my driving test was, for me, one of the most significant moments of my life. For a start, although I had passed exams at school, passing the driving test was a key to successful job applications. Passing the test opened a door to more freedom, it gave me the right to drive on my own, and as I said, being able to drive seemed to be something which the majority of potential employers wanted in an applicant, so it opened doors for me which would otherwise have been shut.

But it did more than that.

Passing my driving test also did something else for ME - it showed me something about tests. It showed ME that I could drive. We don't often consider this, but passing a test (any kind of a test) benefits us, and although often we think about tests being for the benefit of others, actually, one of the best things about a test is that passing it benefits us far more than it does the tester.

It shows us WE can do it.

Passing the driving test showed ME that I could drive.

Passing my surveying exams showed ME that I could be a surveyor.

Completing my basic training and passing my personal weapons test and battle fitness test every year showed me I was a soldier.

Passing a test shows it's that we are capable of doing the thing that we are being tested about.

Thinking about God, thinking about our faith, I want to leave you with this thought: If you are going through a testing time, right now. Whether you have a particular issue you're dealing with, a relationship which is a bit of a burden to you, something in your life that you are thinking "I don't know how much more of this I can take", be encouraged! God KNOWS how much we can take, but often we don't. So perhaps, just perhaps, the test is happening for YOUR benefit, to show YOU that you can do that thing, or endure that thing, or that your faith IS strong enough when you are doubting. Perhaps, you are enduring a test because you need to understand that your faith is stronger than you ever imagined it could be, that it is precious and efficacious and that the other side of the test, you will be more confident in yourself and more assured in your faith.

James writes this about testing ... "*the testing of your faith produces perseverance. Let perseverance finish its work so that you may be mature and complete, not lacking anything.*"[161]

Peter says of tests that they will prove our faith.

And as a final thought, if you think God is silent, don't be discouraged.

The examiner is always silent while the test is in progress.

Satisfaction

Lastly, Philip says to Jesus, "*show us the Father and that will be enough*"[162]. It strikes me that part of our nature is that very often we can never get enough. We have to go further, or get richer, or be faster than the last thing we did. We are driven to always outdo ourselves and one another. We see it regularly on our televisions, shows in series format often do what they describe as "pushing the boundaries" as if that is a good thing, but there is a real lesson here to learn about something being "enough"

The Rolling Stones song: "I can't get no ... satisfaction" is a cry of the age we live in. Many (if not most) people have yet to learn that the deepest yearning inside them cannot be satisfied with stuff or status or anything else this world can give us.

Paul learned that. He said, *"I have learned the secret of being content in each and every circumstance"*[163].

Even as Christians in our churches we sing songs to God that contain lyrics like "You're all I need - you're all I ever wanted", then we go home and we fight and clamour along with the rest of society to get more, to get ahead and by our actions show that we don't really believe what we've sung, we aren't satisfied, we haven't learned Paul's secret. One key to being content in life is to get to a place of being satisfied, and I'm not just talking about physical satisfaction.

There is a sense in which it could be our own fault, Haggai talks of never being satisfied, he says

"You have planted much, but harvested little. You eat, but never have enough. You drink, but never have your fill. You put on clothes, but are not warm. You earn wages, only to put them in a purse with holes in it. [164]

In his prophecy, Haggai says to *pay careful attention to your ways* in v5 and v7.

So, what do we seek for satisfaction, what is it that will be enough for us?

Haggai says in his prophecy that making sure our priorities are right, that putting God first, is key. Philip says something which is very similar, he says *"show us the Father and that will be enough"* Philip didn't say "satisfy my desires" or "make me powerful", he said that the presence of God is the key to being satisfied, and Jesus' response to him is *"anyone who has seen me has seen the Father"*[165]. The writer of Hebrews describes Christ as the *"radiance of God's glory and the exact representation of his being"*[166].

Colossians 1:15 says *"The Son is the image of the invisible God"*, and John says *"No one has ever seen God, but the one and only Son, who is himself God and is in closest relationship with the Father, has made him known"*. [167]

So, If Philip is right in that seeing the Father is enough for us, we can be sure that the most effective way to do that is through Jesus. It is in our own relationship with Jesus where the Father is ultimately revealed to us, so it is in Jesus that our deepest satisfaction lies.

I have heard people say, that because Christians can be content with less and often don't chase after riches like people around them, that they are not ambitious. In fact, I've personally been told that I don't have enough ambition, enough drive in me, that I'm satisfied with too little, and should strive for more.

It is a lie of the devil to make unimportant things seem valuable and to devalue and belittle the richest gains you can experience. Far from settling for less, I would say the opposite is true, people who chase after the things of the world and are satisfied with that, are aiming too low. Why be satisfied with the trinkets of this world when we can gain the riches of heaven in Christ?

6. Bartholomew (Nathanael)

What do we know about Nathanael? Surprisingly, little. In fact, everything we know comes from just two passages in John's Gospel (all other references to him are as a name on a list):

So, Matthew 10:2,3 / Mark 3:18 / Luke 6:14 and Acts 1:13 merely mention Nathanael as one of the 12. We then have a description of his first encounter with Jesus recorded by John at the end of John 1, and his inclusion among the disciples who returned to Galilee recorded at the end of John's gospel.

I want to focus on Nathanael and his conversation with Jesus in John 1:43-50: *"The next day, Jesus decided to leave for Galilee. Finding Philip, he said to him, "Follow me." Philip, like Andrew and Peter, was from the town of Bethsaida. Philip found Nathanael and told him, "We have found the one Moses wrote about in the Law, and about whom the prophets also wrote — Jesus of Nazareth, the son of Joseph." "Nazareth! Can anything good come from there?" Nathanael asked. "Come and see," said Philip. When Jesus saw Nathanael approaching, he said of him, "Here truly is an Israelite in whom there is no deceit." "How do you know me?" Nathanael asked. Jesus answered, "I saw you while you were still under the fig tree before Philip called you." Then Nathanael declared, "Rabbi, you are the Son of God; you are the king of Israel." Jesus said, "You believe because I told you I saw you under the fig tree. You will see greater things than that."*

I want to think about three things which this passage throws up. Two of them come from what Jesus said to Nathanael, and the third comes from Nathanael's response.

1. Jesus says of Nathanael, *"Here truly is an Israelite in whom there is no deceit"*[168]. I want to talk about the importance of the inner man.

2. Related to this, Jesus then says, *"I saw you when you were sitting under the fig tree"*[169]. God sees us in the unseen place.

3. Lastly, I want to talk about Nathanael's description/confession of Jesus, he says, *"Rabbi, you are the Son of God; you are the king of Israel"*[170]. I want to consider what it means that Jesus is our teacher, what the expression "Son of God" tells us about his nature, and how the title King of Israel shows Jesus' authority.

The importance of the inner man

The first thing I want to look at is the first part of Jesus' description of Nathanael. In today's society, there is a focus on externals. How we look, what we say, and how we behave. Our opinions are scrutinised and if we step out of line and act in a way or express a view in public which does not accord to the values of today's society, we can find ourselves in real trouble. Increasingly we have seen in our media programmes stories of some

Christian individual losing their job, or a Christian firm being sued for acting in line with the Bible and not society.

Notwithstanding that, for the moment at least, what we believe and how we think, what we say in private is still our business. We have not yet entered the realms of Brave New World, 1984 or Minority Report where people are accused and sentenced for their thoughts. This is partly because we can not identify what is inside someone unless they reveal it to us through their words or actions. Jesus, however, was not limited in that way. He saw Nathanael in a way no human could. John's gospel tells us that *"when Jesus saw Nathanael approaching, he said of him, 'Here truly is an Israelite in whom there is no deceit'."*[171].

We can often get hung up on human understandings of membership of particular groups of people. When people talk about Israel and Israelites, we have a modern nation state we can look at, and for us, the label Israelite has a similar meaning as saying English, or French or American. Even when we say Jewish, we're talking about a cultural group. When Jesus calls Nathanael a "true Israelite", He is not talking about human descent, He is not even talking about his adherence to a cultural group. He is, rather, talking about what really makes someone an Israelite. Jesus was not talking about Nathanael's works, He wasn't commending him for his good deeds, or the righteous life he led. He wasn't commenting on his public declarations of faith. He isn't even talking about the fact Nathanael told the truth per-se, He was talking about his inner character.

Paul talks of the inner man, he says in Romans 7:22 *"in my inner being I delight in God's law"* and in 2 Corinthians 4:16-18, he places his sense of self-worth entirely on his inner man when he says: *"Therefore we do not lose heart. Though outwardly we are wasting away, yet inwardly we are being renewed day by day. For our light and momentary troubles are achieving for us an eternal glory that far outweighs them all. So, we fix our eyes not on what is seen, but on what is unseen, since what is seen is temporary, but what is unseen is eternal"*. In fact, when we are reborn in the Spirit, Paul describes what happens as a new creation: *"Therefore, if anyone is in Christ, the new creation has come: The old has gone, the new is here!*[172]. Paul isn't talking about a physical transformation in this verse, even though when people come to faith, it is not uncommon for their friends to recognise there's something different and to look for a physical explanation. It's not uncommon for someone to say something like: "there's something different about you, have you had your hair done?" And on some rare occasions, the outward change can be astounding.

But the overwhelming witness of Scripture is that God is far more concerned with our inner person, with our character, than he is with our appearance.

There are a number of other characters in the Bible who are seen for who they are inside....

1. Gideon is hiding from the Midianites, yet he is described as a "mighty warrior".
2. David is called "a man after my heart"
3. Nehemiah describes some of the leaders of Israel as "men of integrity who fear God more than most men do"

One of the most well-known verses which speaks to this is when Samuel looks at Jesse's son Eliab and God says to him, *"Do not consider his appearance or his height, for I have rejected him. The LORD does not look at the things people look at. People look at the outward appearance, but the LORD looks at the heart"*[173]. This is by no means the only place the Scripture shows us that God sees what is in our hearts, and that our position in the kingdom is not by virtue of our actions, but by something much more embedded in our inner man. A lot of the book of Romans tackles this issue, and Paul explains that we, the gentile believers are "grafted" into the people of God through faith [174], and Paul emphasises it clearly to the Ephesians when he writes *"For it is by grace you have been saved, through faith—and this is not from yourselves, it is the gift of God— not by works, so that no one can boast"*[175]. In other words, what is important is not what you do with the outer man, but what happens in the inner man which is important.

John 1:12-13 says, *"Yet to all who did receive him, to those who believed in his name, he gave the right to become* children of God— *children born not of natural descent, nor of human decision or a husband's will, but born of God"*.

Romans 2:28-29, *"A person is not a Jew who is one only outwardly, nor is circumcision merely outward and physical. No, a person is a Jew who is one inwardly; and circumcision is circumcision of the heart, by the Spirit, not by the written code. Such a person's praise is not from other people, but from God"*.

So, although Jesus is clear that how we treat one another is important, these outward expressions of our faith are exactly that. They are expressions of our faith. Our outer actions reveal what is in our inner man.

Jesus says, *"A good man brings good things out of the good stored up in his heart, and an evil man brings evil things out of the evil stored up in his heart"* [176]. It is not without reason that Proverbs says, *"Above all else, guard your heart, for everything you do flows from it"*[177].

Matthew 7:15-20 says, *"Watch out for false prophets. They come to you in sheep's clothing, but inwardly they are ferocious wolves. By their fruit you will recognise them. Do people pick grapes from thorn bushes, or figs from thistles? Likewise, every good tree bears good fruit, but a bad tree bears bad fruit. A good tree cannot bear bad fruit, and a bad tree cannot bear good fruit. Every tree that does not bear good fruit is cut down and thrown into the fire. Thus, by their fruit you will recognise them"*.

He is talking about prophets here, but there is a principle which is true for everyone in this passage: *by their fruit you will recognise them*

In other words, we do not do good things to become Christians. We do good things because we ARE
Christians.

People we talk to will often articulate a belief that
because they do what they think are "good deeds", they
will go to heaven. This shows they believe they are the
ones to determine what is good and bad (instead of
God). They are falling into the trap of believing that it is
those things which make them Christian. This is a disastrous misunderstanding of the Gospel, it puts us and
our actions in the driving seat in determining our suitability for heaven. We are not the judge of all the earth,
God is[178]. We are ingrafted branches, we can know we
are Abraham's spiritual children because of the faith in
our hearts, not the actions of our hands, so Paul can say
Romans 8:14, 16,17 *"those who are led by the Spirit of God
are children of God ... The Spirit himself testifies with our
spirit that we are God's children"*, and *"we are heirs—heirs of
God and co-heirs with Christ"*.

We would do well to remember that!

God sees the unseen

Jesus said to Nathanael, *"I saw you when you were sitting
under the fig tree"*[179]. This point is linked to the above
point. We may feel small and unimportant, but Jesus
notices us.

There have been some very popular television
shows over the years, where a camera is hidden and

secretly records people's reactions when they are put in situations and filmed without their knowledge, but as a general rule, how people act when they think no one is watching or around is very interesting. People's reactions to being filmed or observed without their permission is not always positive, and it can often evoke anger.

Our society also seems interested in and obsessed with the big, the important, and the famous! In fact, years ago if you asked a child what they wanted to do when they get older, you would hear answers like "doctor", "train driver" and the like. Now all kids seem to want to aspire to is being famous. But God is not interested in that stuff, He is interested in the hidden / the unnoticed / the bypassed. Those who the Bible describes as the widow and the foreigner / children / lepers / tax collectors / those collectively called "sinners", etc etc etc. Have you ever felt like no one notices what you do? You feel hidden, unnoticed and therefore, by implication, unimportant? I used to think that whatever I did, there was no point, no one will notice, and no one will care. But Jesus does notice, and He does care.

Jesus notices you. Who you are (and what you do) matters to him. So, Jesus is able to look into Nathanael's character and see the inner man, but he can also see us when we think we are alone. He sees us when we think no one else is watching!

- "Nothing in all creation is hidden from God's sight. Everything is uncovered and laid bare before the eyes of him to whom we must give account"[180].
- "From heaven the LORD looks down and sees all mankind; from his dwelling place he watches all who live on earth — he who forms the hearts of all, who considers everything they do"[181].
- "Your ways are in full view of the LORD, and he examines all your paths"[182].
- (God says:) "My eyes are on all their ways; they are not hidden from me, nor is their sin concealed from my eyes"[183].
- "Am I only a God nearby," declares the LORD, "and not a God far away? Who can hide in secret places so that I cannot see them?" declares the LORD"[184].
- "He reveals deep and hidden things; he knows what lies in darkness, and light dwells with him"[185].

Nathaniel's declaration

Who is Jesus? The answer to this question has eternal implications for us. John records Nathanael answering it like this ... *Rabbi, you are the Son of God; you are the king of Israel* (John 1:49). In other words: I recognise your role (Rabbi = teacher), I recognise your nature (Son of God = divine) and I recognise your authority (king of Israel).

Who is Jesus to us?

Jesus is our TEACHER

In other words, where does our understanding of the things of the world come from? Culture? Reason? Or do we take our cues from God himself? Did Jesus ever call himself Rabbi? No, but he was called Rabbi by people around him. Rabbi is a Hebrew word, not a Greek one, and it simply means "master" or "teacher".

The significance for us today is that if Jesus is our master or teacher, we are accepting a couple of things:

1. **We have something to learn**. In other words, we are not there, we don't have the world sussed, we are not the arbiter of all knowledge. Interestingly, people will often express this view that they see Christians as arrogant people who "think they know it all", yet it is by their actions and not their words, they reveal that the opposite is true, that they think they have the answers. In the same breath, they will say this or something like it, "Who do you think you are to tell me what to do?" In other words, "there's nothing you can teach me, I already have the answers". By contrast, Christians if they are honest recognise that they don't know everything. We are disciples after all and a disciple is "one who learns".

2. **We recognise the place to learn is at the feet of Jesus**. We have reams of teaching from Jesus, and the most precious thing he teaches us is our worth, what He did to rescue us from Sin, and how to appropriate his offer of life for ourselves.

If we could get to the place where like Nathanael, we recognise that the place to be is in the presence of Jesus, that there was something he has to teach us, and that spending time with him is the best way to learn and develop our faith, we would make far fewer mistakes as we walk through life. Hebrews 4:12 says, *"For the word of God is alive and active. Sharper than any double-edged sword, it penetrates even to dividing soul and spirit, joints and marrow; it judges the thoughts and attitudes of the heart."* If we think about the phrase *"the word of God is living and active"* is this about Jesus? (John 1:1 which is clearly about Jesus says, "in the beginning was the word") or is it about the Scripture? Which is it?

This question has had scholars debating and arguing for centuries, but as Charles Spurgeon pointed out, The question actually reveals a great truth because much of what we can say about Jesus we can say about the Bible. Don't forget that the huge bulk of what we know about Jesus is found in the Bible. In other words, the Bible is alive and active because Jesus is in it.

> *God's word will keep you from sin — sin*
> *will keep you from God's word.*

Jesus is DIVINE

Jesus is not just a good man, he is God.

The phrases "son of" and "child of" often[186] denotes a characteristic, so James & John are "sons of thunder" which describes their temper. Joseph of Cyprus was called Barnabas meaning "son of encouragement" which described his character as an encourager. In John 17:12, Jesus' description of Judas is translated as "the one doomed to destruction" in the NIV, but the Greek "huios apōleia" quite literally means "son of destruction" or even "son of hell" (KJV says "son of perdition").

In Matthew 23, Jesus says to the Pharisees *"Woe to you, teachers of the law and Pharisees, you hypocrites! You travel over land and sea to win a single convert, and when you have succeeded, you make them twice as much a child of hell as you are"*[187].

When Nathanael calls Jesus Son of God, he is clearly declaring Jesus' divinity. I think it is very telling that John should record this detail. In fact, the whole purpose of John's gospel is to get us to the place where we recognise and believe this. John starts his gospel declaring *"in the beginning was the word and the word was with God and the word was God"* [188], almost at the end, he tells us the purpose of his gospel *"But these are written that you may believe that Jesus is the Messiah, the Son of God, and that by believing you may have life in his name"*[189].

The progress of people through the Gospel of John shows people who believe in Jesus. Nathanael is, perhaps, the very first person John records doing this.

John's letter is full of references to the Father and his Son Jesus Christ, AND in his letter he says that *"if anyone denies Jesus is the Christ, such a person is the antichrist denying the Father and the Son"*. (the same Greek word is translated as "Christ" here and "Messiah" in John 20:31). Many deny Jesus' divinity. In fact, this is one of the beliefs which sets Christianity apart from all other religions. Christians believe that Christ is divine.

Jesus has AUTHORITY

The declaration by Nathanael that Jesus is the King of Israel is in fact the only confession of Jesus kingship that we find in the Gospels outside the Palm Sunday declarations and Jesus' trial and crucifixion. As Christians, it is fairly common to declare Jesus is our King, but I believe we sometimes miss the significance of what it means when we declare Christ as King.

God's original intent for his people was that they should have no King. So for example Isaiah 43:15, 44:6, Malachi 1:14, Zechariah 14:9 & 4:16-17 all describe God as King, and the implication of this is clearly that His people, Israel, should need no King. So, when we read in the Bible about King David, and Saul and Solomon and all the other Kings, we are reading about something that wasn't part of God's original intent for His people.

The problem, however, was this: Israel got thrashed by the Philistines at the battle of Aphek in BC. 1050. This is a turning point in the history of Israel, and they demand a King. You can read about their demand in 1 Samuel 8:4-9, then 19-22. In 1 Samuel 8:7, God says plainly to Samuel that Israel rejected Him as their King. The people of Israel had really missed the point, they shouldn't have asked for a King, and the fact they did shows us just how far they had turned from God.

The result, then, is that Samuel anoints Saul as King. Saul makes such a pig's ear of being a King that David is chosen. David for all of his love and his heart after God had so much blood on his hands that he was not permitted to complete the temple. His son Solomon also fails as King, and the Kingdom is divided into two kingdoms, Israel (Northern) and Judah (Southern). We then we a succession of Kings in both Kingdoms, some good and some bad, but none of them perfect. And by the time of Jesus, the "King" of the Jews (Herod) was not actually a pure Jew, he was a half-breed (a Jew of Idumean descent), a puppet King, put on the throne by the Romans.

When we think about Jesus as King, we tend to think of the human model of Kingship we see around us. But this is not how God intended to rule as King. I could describe for you all what a King does and what Kingship as we would see it means, but I believe that this is a poor reflection of God's intention as our King. In fact, John 6:15 describes Jesus withdrawing because he knew the people wanted to make him King, and in John 18:36 He says this:

"My Kingdom is not of this world. If it were, my servants would fight to prevent my arrest by the Jews. But now my Kingdom is from another place."

If, then, we restrict our understanding of Jesus' Kingship to that which we see in earthly Kings, then we are missing something. I want to consider how Jesus truly fulfils his function of King. Jesus's kingdom is …

1. Neither Temporal nor Geographical

Ephesians 1:20-22, Matthew 18:28, 1 Corinthians 15:25. Jesus' Kingship is not about physical, geographical areas, it is, as Paul says, *"far above all rule authority, and power and dominion"*[190]. We also tend to think in terms of the future when we think of Jesus as King, especially when we look at passages like Revelation 15:3, 17:14 and 19:16, which put Christ's Kingship into the future, but Christ won't be the King of Kings, he IS the King of Kings.

We live in a world that is full of chaos and turmoil. Over the last few years we've seen dictators fall, we've seen uprisings and struggles for geographical or political power, and we'll see more as the years progress. We need to constantly be aware as we look at these things on our TVs that our King is above all these things.

2. Not about Power or Status

Human role models look for authority, power and status, but the role model we have for Kingship is quite different. Jesus does not lord it over us, he does not follow the modern, or indeed any human example of Kingship, and His example of Kingship is one of a servant. The key passage here, I believe, is Philippians 2:6ff

3. Not about Force

The Jews of Jesus' day were sick of being under the

rule of Rome, they were looking for a leader, a King who would overthrow the Romans and usher in a new time of victory and prosperity for the nation. They looked back to the Kingdoms of David and Solomon and the King they were looKing for was a King from out of the same mould, a King who would give them political victory, victory in battle, victory over their enemies, the oppressors of God's people. This is why I believe they were caught up in the moment of that day: they wanted a release.

The Bible says in John 6 that Jesus withdrew from the crowds because He knew that they intended to make him King by force [191].

That is not the way Jesus works. He will come to you, He will speak truth into your heart and your life, but whether you act on that truth is entirely YOUR choice. Christ will live as King in your life only when you choose to make him king.

Far too often we claim to be Christians, and then live as if our King is not our King. We are either subjects of the King of Kings, and citizens of his Kingdom, or we are not. Jesus will not take my life and force obedience like an earthly King, He asks for it, he deserves it, but he will not force it on me. If there is an element of your life where you feel that Christ is not victorious, it is possible that you have not yet made him King there. Just as Jesus refused to win the earth by force, he refuses to force his way into our lives, or the lives of people around us.

Concluding thoughts

1. Since we know that it is our inner man and not our outer actions which define who we are, and ultimately are what has eternal significance, is it not important that we deal with the things inside us?

2. How do you respond when you realise that God can see you even in the hidden place? When you know God sees your very character?

   Do you shrink from the light because you hate the darkness?[192]

   Or, like Nathanael, do you respond with love and faith?

3. Do you dismiss the bible out of hand because it was written by men thousands of years ago? By men who have little or no concept of life in the 21st century? Or do you accept it as the word of God, as living and active, and God breathed, and useful for (as Paul says to Timothy) *"teaching, rebuking, correcting and training in righteousness"*[193].

4. Do we live like Jesus is our king? I mean, really live? People who live in the UK complain, and moan, and recently, we've even seen them riot. They live as citizens of our nation, but they live with contempt for our laws and for our way of government, and in some cases for our way of life. Is that how you live as a Christian? Do you claim to be a citizen of heaven, but kick against the implications that brings? *"Since you died with Christ to the elemental spiritual forces of this world, why, as though you still*

belonged to the world, do you submit to its rules?"[194]._ "We are those who have died to sin; how can we live in it any longer?"_[195].

7. Thomas (Didymus, the twin)

Thomas is also called Didymus,[196] which means "twin". Whether he was quite literally a twin, or whether it was just a name given to him, we just don't know. If he did have a twin, we know nothing about him, which raises some interesting questions about why not.

I only mention this because it is tempting to draw spiritual lessons from things we infer from the Bible text rather than from what it actually says. As a general rule, I would say that it is wise to steer clear of, or at the very least be wary of any statement of faith or doctrine made because of an inference or implication in Scripture without recognising that it is actually not explicitly stated.

What the Bible actually says about Thomas.

That said, let's look at what Scripture says about Thomas. There are some references to Thomas as part of the larger group of the disciples. He is included in the lists of the disciples, and he is also named as one of the 6 disciples who went fishing with Peter in John 21. He did ask Jesus a question which triggered one of the "I am" statements of Jesus. In John 14:5: *"Thomas said to him, 'Lord, we don't know where you are going, so how can we* know the way?'" Jesus response is *"I am the way, the truth and the life"*. I am not going to tackle this particular exchange here. There is a temptation to try to cover everything in these studies, but I want to focus on the other two specific references to Thomas and his interactions with Jesus.

One is where Thomas speaks out as the disciples are considering the reception that they will get if they go to Bethany after the news about Lazarus's death has reached them. The second is the interaction with the disciples and Jesus for which Thomas is most well known, his statement which earned him the title "doubting Thomas".

Courage and Fear.

John 11:16: *"Then Thomas (also known as Didymus) said to the rest of the disciples, 'Let us also go, that we may die with him'"*. This reveals courage in the face of fear, or at least a belief that this action will result in death and a willingness to face that end. Did the disciples really believe that they would be killed? — The text doesn't tell us, John merely records Thomas's words.

I see a parallel with Peter's declaration *"I will never leave you Lord even if it means I will die"*[197] and as Jesus is arrested, tied and executed, Peter fails to live up to his declaration, though ultimately he will follow through and be martyred. Thomas on the other hand convinces the other disciples to go to Bethany.

What are we to take home from this?

Fear and Courage. The disciples were aware of, or at least had an anticipation, that they would not be welcomed into Bethany. They articulate in John 11:8 *"But Rabbi,"* they said, *"a short while ago the Jews there tried to stone you, and yet you are going back?"*. Were they afraid? I would have been. Jesus is clear that there will be things to fear in this world, but he warns us to be sure we are fearful of the right things, or rather, not to be fearful of things we don't need to fear. He says in Matthew 10:28 *"Do not be afraid of those who kill the body but cannot kill the soul. Rather, be afraid of the One who can destroy both soul and body in hell"* and Luke 12:4,5 record his words as well: *"I tell you, my friends, do not be afraid of those who kill the body and after that can do no more. But I will show you whom you should fear: Fear him who, after your body has been killed, has authority to throw you into hell. Yes, I tell you, fear him"*.

Jesus also says to the disciples in John 16:33 that *"in this world you will have troubles, but take heart I have overcome the world"* (note that in the first half of the verse, he declares that our peace is to be found in him). He has earlier expounded on this in John 15:18-21. 1 Peter 3:14 says, *"but even if you should suffer for what is right, you are blessed. 'Do not fear their threats; do not be frightened'"*.

The point here is that following Jesus is far from the "crutch" that people think it is. In fact, choosing to follow Jesus in the face of the anti-Christian indoctrination and ridicule and social pressures we have around us is about as far from conforming as you can get. Choosing to be a bible-believing Christian means that the things you will accept about people, about marriage and sexuality and the value you place on human life (especially unborn human life) will put you at loggerheads with nearly everyone you meet.

Anyone who is a Christian really must consider where their faith will lead them. We truly must take up our cross and follow him. Dietrich Bonhoeffer, the pastor executed by the Nazis in the last days of World War 2 is very blunt in his book "Cost of Discipleship" about this. We must not live under cheap grace, he says. We must understand everything that following Jesus implies, up to and including death. This is the overwhelming witness of Scripture from Jesus own words about the world hating us and taking up our cross, through Paul asserting that following Jesus means we will have to give up all things and become like Christ, Hebrews describing the heroes of the faith and the troubles they went through, Peter says we will be persecuted for our faith, as does James. Again and again, the New Testament tells us that we will be persecuted for our faith. And finally in Revelation, the second half of 12:11 says *"they did not love their lives so much as to shrink from death"*. In the 21st Century many think that they won't be killed for the faith, but increasingly the Christian faith is being seen as incompatible with modern society which is becoming antagonistic towards people who hold to it. The only truly humanistic societies in our world, the communist nations both past and present have appalling human rights records, ESPECIALLY toward Christians, so I don't want to be a harbinger of doom, but that kind of persecution and hate is just around the corner again for Christians in modern societies.

It is already a reality for Christians all over the world, for example in North Korea, China, numerous countries in the Middle East, and in the Far East. It is also becoming increasingly common in India, Pakistan and any one of a number of other "anti-Christian" nations.

I suggest you look at the organisation Open Doors, which will give more details to inform your prayer lives.

Doubt and Faith

The second thing I want to unpack comes from the most well-known account of Thomas, the one which earns him the reputation of "doubting Thomas".

" *Now Thomas (also known as Didymus), one of the Twelve, was not with the disciples when Jesus came. So the other disciples told him, "We have seen the Lord!"*
But he said to them, "Unless I see the nail marks in his hands and put my finger where the nails were, and put my hand into his side, I will not believe."
A week later his disciples were in the house again, and Thomas was with them. Though the doors were locked, Jesus came and stood among them and said, "Peace be with you!" Then he said to Thomas, "Put your finger here; see my hands. Reach out your hand and put it into my side. Stop doubting

and believe."

Thomas said to him, "My Lord and my God!"

Then Jesus told him, "Because you have seen me, you have believed; blessed are those who have not seen and yet have believed"[198]

This is the account for which Thomas is most remembered, in fact it is this characteristic of Thomas which has so informed our culture that anyone who looks with any skepticism about something that they are given the title which I've already used: "doubting Thomas". But we must note this: none of the disciples believed Jesus was raised until he appeared to them. The women at the tomb believed, but the disciples we are told *"did not believe the women because their words seemed to them like nonsense"*[199], and again Matthew records that the disciples meet Jesus at the shores of Galilee and Matthew records that *"when they saw him, they worshiped him; but some doubted"*[200].

For the last three years, all the disciples had witnessed and shared in Jesus ministry. They had been there when Jesus raised Lazarus from the dead, they were there at the last supper when Jesus predicts his death. Then their world had fallen apart. They had seen their leader arrested and tried and executed, they had all fled in terror and they were expecting a knock on the door from the authorities at any moment. This is a chaotic time for the disciples, and emotionally and mentally they must have been all over the place. And then the women come back from the tomb with an incredible story — that Jesus has risen.

What would you have done?

So although Thomas is the one tarred with the reputation of being the doubter, he is not alone. Either then, or now. None of the disciples had believed, Thomas was the only one honest enough to articulate it. All Christians suffer doubt at one time or another, but the example of doubting Thomas provides both instruction and encouragement.

So how do we keep from doubting as Thomas did? Here are just a couple of thoughts to help you.

Firstly, one of the most significant things which we know from this account is right at the start, *"Now Thomas ... was not with the disciples when Jesus came"*. The first point I want to make is this: If you are not there, you will miss out!

I have lost count of the number of times that something has happened and I've missed it because I wasn't there. For Thomas, this is significant, because he missed seeing the resurrected Christ along with the others, and it was this missing out which was articulated in his expression of doubt. Having said that, one remedy to or defence against doubt is the fellowship of the church, the writer to the Hebrews tells us that the fellowship "spurs us on" towards love and good works[201], and that it is a source of encouragement.

If we absent ourselves from our fellow Christians, we are almost certainly going to experience higher levels of doubt in our faith. It is counter-intuitive I know, because when we feel low in our faith, our first instinct it to withdraw from church, but this is the very moment we should make the effort and join in with our fellow believers.

Ecclesiastes says that *"Two are better than one, because they have a good return for their labour: If either of them falls down, one can help the other up. But pity anyone who falls and has no one to help them up. Also, if two lie down together, they will keep warm. But how can one keep warm alone? Though one may be overpowered, two can defend themselves. A cord of three strands is not quickly broken"*[202]. This is not immediately a verse which comes to mind when thinking about doubt and the role of fellowship, but it does show how important others are when we are weak or stumble and need help. We so often think of this verse in practical terms, but I would suggest that other people can also help us carry our faith. Just as we carry bags for our children until they are old enough to carry them for themselves, just as when someone sustains an injury and we do what we can to assist them physically until they are healed, I venture to suggest that as we fellowship, one of the greatest strengths and joys of being in fellowship is this corporate carrying of one another's burdens. Fellowship with others is key for us in maintaining our faith.

But we do have a tension here, Jesus words to Thomas seems to cut across this. Thomas, having missed out, articulates *"I won't believe unless I see for myself"*. Jesus didn't have to reveal himself to Thomas, but he did, and Thomas believed. However, Jesus says to Thomas something which reaches across time and declares that we are blessed, he says *"Because you have seen* me, you have believed; blessed are those who have not seen and yet have believed". That is us, today, that Jesus is talking about. Like Thomas we have not seen the risen Christ physically, but we believe, and Christ declares us blessed. So whilst it is incredibly important, and a real antidote to doubt, personal experience is not absolutely essential to faith. It is possible to believe in Jesus even though we have not seen him. In fact in Hebrews 11:1, one of the best descriptions of faith we have, we read *"faith is confidence in what we hope for and assurance about what we do not see"*. And this same thought is reinforced by Peter who writes this: *"Though you have not seen him, you love him; and even though you do not see him now, you believe in him and are filled with an inexpressible and glorious joy, for you are receiving the end result of your faith, the salvation of your souls"*[203]. I have not personally touched Jesus physically, he has not eaten with me — yet. But Jesus words to Thomas stretch through time and promise us who believe that we are blessed! Wow what a promise.

The second point I want to make about doubt is that it is not a consistent thing. Doubt rises and falls in us, sometimes our faith seems strong and at other times, doubt crowds in and it it feels like we've lost it all together. James talks about doubt, in James 1, talking about prayer, he says this, *"But when you ask, you must believe and not doubt, because the one who doubts is like a wave of the sea, blown and tossed by the wind. That person should not expect to receive anything from the Lord"*[204]. Doubt is rarely intellectual. It is more frequently an emotional response to circumstances than it is a thought out response to an argument.

Jesus also talks about doubt and the effect it has on prayer, in both Matthew and Mark, he says that one of the keys to our effectiveness is that we don't doubt, so for example, taking Matthew's gospel, we read, *"Jesus replied, "Truly I tell you, if you have faith and do not doubt, not only can you do what was done to the fig tree, but also you can say to this mountain, 'Go, throw yourself into the sea,' and it will be done"*[205].

So doubt is a problem in the life of a believer. I want to make one comment which may seem odd, but just bear with me as I try to articulate it — Doubt is not possible without faith. What I mean by that is that if you don't believe, you are not a doubter, you are an unbeliever. Doubt can only exist in the presence of faith. Unlike an unbeliever, a doubter is open to the possibility of faith, so if you are experiencing doubt, be encouraged! If you are experiencing doubt, you haven't lost your faith at all. Note also that James says that doubt is like a wave of the sea, and to steal from a metaphor I heard about something else, for many people, doubt and faith are like two wolves fighting inside us for dominance, and as has been said, the one which wins is the one you feed. Mark records that on one occasion, a man brought his son to Jesus who was afflicted by a demon, and during the interaction between Jesus and the man, Jesus says *"everything is possible for one who believes"*, the man's response is *"I do believe, help my unbelief!"*[206]

Finally

First, we must recognise that Christians fight a spiritual battle daily. We have to gear up for the battle. Doubt is a spiritual attack, it is something which we must defend ourselves against. Do not see doubt as a weakness or deficiency in you, it is an attack which comes from the enemy.

Second, the antidote to doubt is faith, so building our faith is a powerful defence against doubt, and we can do this by:

1. Feeding on the word of God. Paul writes that faith comes by hearing and hearing by the word of God[207], Times of doubt will become less frequent if we take advantage of the good times to feed our faith with the Word of God. Then when we raise the shield of faith and do battle with the enemy of our souls, his flaming darts of doubt will not hit their target.

2. The next thing we can do when doubt attacks us is to go to God in prayer. Like the man who brought his demon possessed child to Jesus but was unsure whether Jesus could help him, we go to God because we believe in Him and ask Him for more and greater faith to overcome our doubts.

3. Lastly, at the very least, it makes good sense to stay in fellowship with other Christians. I have met people on numerous occasions who for one reason or another leave a church, and rather than seeking out fellowship, stay isolated. Overwhelmingly such

people find that their doubt increases, their faith wanes and eventually they drift away from it altogether.

So the message of Thomas is this, you do not need to be derailed by doubt!

8. Matthew (Levi) the Tax collector

You would have thought that the disciple who gave his name to the first Gospel in the New Testament would be well known to us, that we would have loads of information about him, that there would be lots of references to him in all the gospel accounts. But that is not what we find. There are only 7 Bible references to Matthew: His call (recorded in the synoptic Gospels), and his inclusion in the lists of the apostles (synoptic Gospels and Acts). Matthew does not appear at all in John's gospel.

"As Jesus went on from there, he saw a man named Matthew sitting at the tax collector's booth. "Follow me," he told him, and Matthew got up and followed him"[208].

"As he walked along, he saw Levi son of Alphaeus sitting at the tax collector's booth. "Follow me," Jesus told him, and Levi got up and followed him"[209].

"After this, Jesus went out and saw a tax collector by the name of Levi sitting at his tax booth. "Follow me," Jesus said to him, and Levi got up, left everything and followed him. Then Levi held a great banquet for Jesus at his house, and a large crowd of tax collectors and others were eating with them"[210].

You will have noticed that Matthew is called Levi in Mark and Luke[211], and Mark tells us he is the son of Alphaeus. James the son of Alphaeus is also listed among the Apostles[212]. If it is the same Alphaeus, which seems likely, this suggests that Matthew and James were brothers like James and John, and Peter and Andrew. I am not going to say anything more about this here, but it is interesting to note that three sets of brothers appear to be in the group of disciples, and other Bible evidence shows us that faith can so often run like a vein of gold through a family. Don't be discouraged if you have family who are not believers. Pray for them and see what God will do.

Early church writings suggest that Matthew travelled to Ethiopia, where he became associated with Candace, identified with the eunuch of Acts 8:27. Those accounts tell us of Matthew's martyrdom in that country.

Matthew was a tax collector

Jesus called a tax collector to be an apostle. I sometimes think the significance of this and the impact it would have had on the people around him is lost on us. To the Jews, tax collectors were the lowest of the low. They represented an occupying force, and its ability to control the people. They had a reputation for being greedy and dishonest, and they would have been viewed with the same hatred that collaborators were during the Second World War.

When we read the gospels, just notice how frequently the phrase "tax collectors and sinners" occurs. Have you ever thought about that? They weren't even considered to be deserving of association with sinners! No self-respecting Jew would ever associate with a tax collector, the only friends a tax collector would have would be other tax collectors. And yet ...

Jesus often initiated contact with those people who were outcast by society: lepers, publicans, sinners, prostitutes. Jesus not only forgave sinners, he openly associated with them, even though it meant that he was criticised for it. Tax collectors seem to be in a category all of their own.

On one occasion, Jesus says this: *"Truly I tell you, the tax collectors and the prostitutes are entering the kingdom of God ahead of you. For John came to you to show you the way of righteousness, and you did not believe him, but the tax collectors and the prostitutes did. And even after you saw this, you did not repent and believe him"*[213]. In other words, he was saying to his listeners "the tax collectors and sinners are entering heaven before you are"!

We read about three tax collectors in the gospels ...

1. Zacchaeus. He was a short man who Jesus chose to eat with. Zacchaeus was so touched by Jesus, he changed. In fact, so much so, he promises to pay back 4 times anything he has cheated from people. Jesus declares, *"today salvation has come to this house!"* You can read the Bible's account of this in Luke 19:1-9. There is a saying which says you can tell what is important to someone in two ways. What do they give their time to? What do they give

their money to? One of the marks of true salvation, I would suggest is that it affects our purse strings.

2. Jesus tells a parable to contrast self-righteousness with true repentance, and uses a tax collector and a pharisee to do so. In Luke 18:9-14, He declared that the tax collector who truly repented was justified when the Pharisee was not. This unnamed tax collector teaches us that true repentance is found in the heart. It works out in our daily lives, it is seen in our actions and in our words, but ultimately, what is seen comes from within, from our heart attitudes. That is what the sermon on the mount is all about. But we must be wary of believing that it is our actions which make us Christian. When we do that, we become like the Pharisee in this parable.

3. Jesus chooses Matthew, a tax collector, to be one of his disciples. That Jesus would do this would have been shocking to those around him, not least the other disciples! Matthew immediately left his tax booth and followed Jesus. True faith is in the inner man, it affects our pockets, and ultimately, it is seen in our lives. Baptism is an outward sign of an inner change. True faith means leaving the old life behind and living a new life in Jesus. Jesus says Luke 9:62 *"No one who puts a hand to the plough and looks back is fit for service in the kingdom of God."* When Matthew left his booth to follow Christ, his commitment was total, and it was permanent.

Why? Why associate with and commend people who society at large, let alone "the righteous" wants nothing to do with?

Some teach that if we are to remain pure as Christians, then it is better not to associate with the world. But for Jesus, this would be a false thing. Jesus doesn't see what people are, but what they could be. He doesn't pigeonhole them according to what they are, what they have done, or where they have come from. He looks beyond what they are to the potential they have in God. You do not compromise holiness when you relate with a sinner. On the contrary, holiness is characterised by the way it reaches out in mercy to others. God can take and totally transform a sinner who is responsive to Him. On the other hand, the most righteous and Holy person, who is not responsive to God, is useless to Him.

The first truth of the Gospel is that Jesus does not follow our ways of evaluating people.

It seems to me that people when presented with the Gospel fall into one of two categories:

Firstly. Many people will adopt the narrative of modern society which asserts that "sin" (whatever it is) is in the eye of the beholder, that every person is capable of and responsible for individually determining what sin is. As long as I don't hurt anyone by my actions, the argument goes, no one has the right to impose their morality on me. In fact, it is not uncommon for people to get very upset and say things like "how dare you judge me!", then those same people will vigorously attack and criticise people who have opinions, values and now even ancestors which are not in line with their own assessments of what is right and wrong, what is good and bad. In our modern society, the assessment of whether something is sin or not is determined not by the Bible, not by the word of God, but by personal or group opinion.

Secondly. People may well accept the existence of morality beyond personal opinion, and they may even understand and assent to God. They will, however, when presented with the message of the Gospel, reject it because they have believed the lie that we have to live in such a way as to deserve the forgiveness that Jesus. They will articulate it something like this:

"you don't know what I've done", "I'm beyond help", or "God can't (won't) forgive me".

This is a disastrous misunderstanding of the nature of God, the power of the cross and truth of the Gospel. Jesus' inclusion of Matthew, a tax collector, one of the despised and hated in society teaches us this:

"… the vilest offender who truly believes, that moment from Jesus a pardon receives" ("To God be the Glory" by Charles Wesley). "Amazing Grace" writer, the reformed slave trader John Newton said this in his later life "Although my memory's fading, I remember two things very clearly: I am a great sinner and Christ is a great Saviour."

Interestingly, if you read the book "The Cross and the Switchblade" which is a testimony by David Wilkerson about his work among the gangs in New York, you will read his account of an encounter with gang member

Nicky Cruz. Nicky had threatened to kill him, and in his book he recalls that event ...

"You could do that, you could cut me in a thousand pieces and lay them out in the street and every piece would love you." But as I said it, I was thinking: and it wouldn't be a bit of good — not with you, Nicky — there's no love on earth that could reach you" (The Cross and the Switchblade ch 7).

We so often make assessments of each other. We must understand that God's assessment of them is not ours! Jesus' choosing of Matthew speaks right into this, as does God's choice of all sorts of people:

1. Cyrus, king of Persia. A foreign pagan king who cannot be more ungodly is described by God through the prophet Isaiah as "my shepherd", and as his "anointed" [214].

2. Jesus references Naaman the Syrian and the widow in Zarepath, both of whom are gentiles [215].

3. Jesus stops and talks to a Samaritan, not just a Samaritan, but a Samaritan woman, and a loose Samaritan woman at that! [216].

4. He tells a parable about a Samaritan man to show the Jews how to act in a neighbourly way [217].

5. He says of a Roman centurion that he has never seen such faith as his in the whole of Israel [218].

Don't rely on society to inform you as to who has value in God's eyes and who doesn't!

Don't believe that your own personal assessment of

your value is anything like God's.

Don't allow others to dictate to you what your value is either.

You need to know this.

Jesus loves you, and He died for you. He says to you, *"come and follow me"*[219], and there is nothing in your background or in your reputation which can stop you from following that call and knowing his peace in your heart. Unless you let it.

Matthew was rich

The Bible doesn't specify that Matthew was rich, but he was a tax collector, and given what we know about tax collectors in Jesus' day, it is highly unlikely he was poor!

When people talk about Jesus and Christians, there is often a focus on the poor, on Jesus's and God's concern for the poor, on those who are unable to care for themselves. It is not without reason that God calls the people of Israel to care for the fatherless and the widow, two examples of people who are totally and completely unable to provide for themselves. The Torah is replete with laws that call Israel to provide for those who cannot provide for themselves. Concern for the poor is a **GOOD** thing! I say this now because I don't want you to misunderstand what I am about to say.

One consequence of a focus on the poor is the belief that God prefers poor people above everyone else. Most notably, it is shown in an understanding of Christianity called liberation theology, which believes that wealth should be redistributed to the poor (with the use of lethal force if necessary).

However, if we set aside our bias towards the poor and really read the gospels, at times Jesus seems to positively favour those who are not poor. Many among Jesus friends and first followers were not poor by the standards of His day. James and John (as we have noted previously) lived in a family which was wealthy enough to have hired men working for them. Joseph of Arimathea and Nicodemus were both religious leaders, and both would have been wealthy, and both followed Jesus. Tax collectors were certainly not poor, yet Jesus seemed to spend lots of time with them.

The issue for Jesus was not wealth in or of itself, but our attitude towards it. One of the most misquoted bible verses is *"**the love of** money is the root of all evil"*[220], which is frequently quoted as *"money is the root of all evil"*. There is a real level of ambivalence towards wealth and wealthy Christians in the Christian community. Too often, we have distort things and view people who have wealth as somehow less deserving of Jesus than those who are poor, almost to the point of regarding wealthy Christians as pariahs and traitors to the faith. But the Jewish law itself says, *"Do not pervert justice; do not show partiality to the poor or favouritism to the great, but judge your neighbour fairly"*[221] . In other words, neither poverty, nor riches should influence the value we place on people. "Love of money" is not an attitude peculiar to the wealthy, in fact poor people are often more occupied with the accumulation of personal wealth than wealthy ones are.

And that is the point I want to make.

1. When wealth and its accumulation takes the place that God should have in our lives, this is a problem for Jesus.
2. Wealth can provide security for us, yet Jesus teaches our security should be in God.
3. Wealth can provide status, but Jesus says that we should not fight for status like people do.
4. Wealth makes us feel significant, and Jesus says your significance come from God's love for you.
5. Wealth gives us the ability to increase our possessions. Jesus says that our earthly possessions are of no eternal value. You can take your stuff to heaven when you die, but it will be destroyed by fire when you get there[222].

Wealth in and of itself is not wrong, but far too often it can get in the way of our relationship with God, which is why Jesus challenged the rich young man to sell all his possessions and follow him[223]. Matthew did exactly that, he abandoned the comforts of this life because he had found something far more valuable than all the world's riches.

The question each and every one of us must answer for ourselves is how precious are our possessions to us? Do we see our possessions as ours? In the description of the fellowship of believers in Acts says *"No one claimed that any of their possessions was their own, but they shared everything they had"* [224]. When the building of the temple started, David said: *"LORD our God, all this abundance that we have provided for building you a temple for your Holy Name **comes from your hand, and all of it belongs to you**. I know, my God, that you test the heart and are pleased with integrity. All these things I have given willingly and with honest intent. And now I have seen with joy how willingly your people who are here have given to you:*[225].

Paul says that all things come from God, *"for us there is but one God, the Father, from whom all things came"*[226].

When we realise none of our wealth and possessions really belongs to us, but come from and ultimately belong to God, it transforms our attitude towards them, so Paul can say, *"whatever were gains to me, I now consider loss for the sake of Christ. What is more, I consider everything a loss because of the surpassing worth of knowing Christ Jesus my Lord, for whose sake I have lost all things. I consider them garbage, that I may gain Christ"*[227]. Paul is not just talking about money here, he is also talking about the other things we chase, things like status, power, influence, reputation as well. But the principle holds for possessions as well. Peter articulates it like this: trials come *"so that the proven genuineness of your faith—of greater worth than gold, which perishes even though refined by fire—*

may result in praise, glory and honour when Jesus Christ is revealed"[228] he is saying that our faith is more valuable than any amount of riches!

This point from Matthew is that we must get our priorities right, wealth is a resource for us to use for his kingdom, not a target for us to aim at. We must value faith, value people and use wealth, not the other way around.

Matthew left his booth

We read that when Jesus called Matthew, he left his booth and followed him. Matthew Immediately left his booth to follow Jesus.

1. He left the old life behind
2. He did it straight away, no hesitation.

Leaving the old life.

Jesus says a number of things about leaving the old life. He says: *"no one who looks back to the plough is fit for service"*[229], and *"go and sell all your possessions, give your money to the poor and then come follow me"*[230].

He even talks about leaving family. He says: *"Anyone who loves their father or mother more than me is not worthy* of me; anyone who loves their son or daughter more than me is not worthy of me. Whoever does not take up their cross and follow me is not worthy of me"[231].

The point here is that one of the biggest barriers to faith is the love of our current life and an unwillingness to leave it behind.

To illustrate this, my friend Dave (not his real name) had in the past been a Christian, but sadly as is all too common, he had drifted away from the church and from Jesus, and when I was working with him, he had no intention of ever being a Christian again. After a couple of years working alongside him, and talking to him, I remember one occasion when he said this "I know that following Jesus again is the right thing to do, and that I should do it. The problem is that I know there are some things in my life which are not compatible with doing that and frankly, I am not ready to give them up. I don't WANT to".

Dave understood that to authentically follow Jesus, there are things which we all enjoy which are incompatible with our faith, which we must leave behind. Certain habits and attitudes, actions and things in our lifestyles which we have to get rid of. Many people are like Dave, they are not prepared to pay the price of peace with God.

Paul was in that place, but when confronted by the Saviour, the choice he made was to pay that price. Looking back on all the things he used to do, the type of person he was, he can reflect on them and say *"But whatever were gains to me, I now consider loss for the sake of Christ. What is more, I consider everything a loss because of the surpassing worth of knowing Christ Jesus my Lord, for whose sake I have lost all things. I consider them garbage, that I may gain Christ"*[232].

"Immediately".

Matthew did not hesitate to follow Jesus. Interestingly the people who hesitate in the Gospels are those who have something to lose, either materially, or in terms of social standing. So for example, the rich young man who came to Jesus and asked what he must do to be saved, had too strong a love of his wealth and his status, so he went away sad. We have the description of people who say to Jesus "I will follow you Lord, but first ..." So for example, in Luke 9:59-62, *"Jesus said to another man, "Follow me." But he replied, "Lord, first let me go and bury my father." Jesus said to him, "Let the dead bury their own dead, but you go and proclaim the kingdom of God." Still another said, "I will follow you, Lord; but first let me go back and say goodbye to my family." Jesus replied, "No one who puts a hand to the plow and looks back is fit for service in the kingdom of God."*

"Almost an Angel" is a secular film in which the actor Paul Hogan plays a man who dies and is sent back as an angel for a second chance at being good. Setting aside the ridiculous idea that angels are dead people sent back to help humans in need (which couldn't be more unbiblical if it tried), ignoring how the film portrays what he sees after he has died, and how God is portrayed (by Charlton Heston), it makes a number of very interesting comments on faith, the church and spirituality in general. One thing which Paul Hogan's character says is, "I was planning to get religious right before I died". This is the default of so many people all over the world, but the massive weakness of this approach is that no one knows when they are going to die! The only way to be sure is to come to Christ NOW.

There will come a time when it is too late to follow the Lord, Even though Scripture tells us that *"The Lord is not slow in keeping his promise, as some understand slowness. Instead, he is patient with you, not wanting anyone to perish, but everyone to come to repentance"*[233], the very next verse says that when he comes it will be swift and unexpected, and it will be too late for those who have refused: *"the day of the Lord will come like a thief. The heavens will disappear with a roar; the elements will be destroyed by fire, and the earth and everything done in it will be laid bare"*[234]. As Augustine said in the third century "it's never too early to come to Christ, but at any moment it could be too late"

Matthew threw a party

"Then Levi held a great banquet for Jesus at his house, and a large crowd of tax collectors and others were eating with

them"[235]. Interestingly, Jesus' interaction with Zacchaeus also centred around a meal.

When we see heaven portrayed on our televisions, we most frequently see it shown as some kind of bland colourless ethereal place, harps playing in the background, everyone dressed in white. There is little or no atmosphere. Christians, however, don't see heaven like that. The most common metaphor for heaven I hear Christians use is that of worship, almost like the best, most wonderful worship service we have ever experienced. However, the most common picture of heaven the New Testament paints, and the one Jesus uses most, is that of a party or a feast! Neither of which is bland and colourless!

The image of feasting crops up all over the Scriptures:

The parable of the great banquet in Luke 14:15-24 describes heaven as a great feast, and the king (God) sending an invitation out to all who will come. The parable of the wise and foolish virgins, which describes a great wedding banquet. Revelation also describes heaven as a banquet, *"Then the angel said to me, "Write this: Blessed are those who are invited to the wedding supper of the Lamb!" And he added, "These are the true words of God"*[236].

Isaiah describes being in the presence of God in this way: *"On this mountain the LORD Almighty will prepare a feast of rich food for all peoples, a banquet of aged wine—the best of meats and the finest of wines"*[237]. Luke 13:29 tells us that people will come from east and west and north and south, and will take their places at the feast in the kingdom of God.

David describes God preparing a table for him in the presence of his enemies[238].

In Revelation 3:20 John records Jesus saying *"Here I am! I stand at the door and knock. If anyone hears my voice and opens the door, I will come in and eat with that person, and they with me"*. Note, "eating" depicts relationship and fellowship. Heaven will be a banquet, a celebration, a party!

Jesus describes rejoicing in heaven whenever a sinner comes to faith [239], and our eternity will be a blast!

The great news is this ... ALL are invited

So, the question we must each answer for ourselves is, "have YOU accepted the invitation?"

9. James the Less

I'm going to start by describing something many of us went through at school. This happened in our sports lessons and it also happened during our break times.

Whenever a team game was played, two people were chosen to be captains and all the other players would line up and the captains would take turns at choosing players to be on their team. It was always immediately apparent who the popular kids were. They got picked first, even before people who were actually good at whatever sport it was (in my school anyway). We lived in fear of being picked last, of being the unpopular, invisible one.

Many of us can identify with being the invisible one at school. I wasn't the best at anything. I wasn't in any school teams, I didn't win any awards, I wasn't a brain-box or geek and great at my studies, but I wasn't a numpty either. I just muddled along in the middle. I was invisible, and I kept my head down as best I could and endured it.

One of the disciples, one of the 12 men personally selected by Jesus to carry his message of hope to the world is all but unknown to us. He is the embodiment of the unknown, invisible one.

This man is James. But not James the brother of John, not James the brother of Jesus, but a shadowy figure few people can remember if asked to list the 12 Disciples. This man is James, son of Alphaeus, or more commonly known as James the Less. The inclusion of his name in the lists of the Disciples, and the inference that he was, along with all the other Disciples, witness to all that Jesus said and did is practically all we know about him. James the less, if he ever did anything to stand out from the other Apostles, if he ever asked Jesus a question worthy of note, Scripture does not record it. Practically everything he ever did or said is lost to history.

The only thing about James which stands out is that he does not stand out, he is completely obscure. He even has a common name.

But don't forget that he is not called "the less" because he is less important! He is called the less because we know less about him.

He was a disciple, and Jesus loved all of the disciples. He taught them all, they all spent three years with him, and they were all present and involved in the establishing and growth of the early church.

James the Less saw the risen Christ. He received the gift of the Holy Spirit in that upper room in Jerusalem and along with the other disciples burst out into the streets at 9 in the morning praising God.

The witness of the early church fathers was that he was thrown down from the temple in Jerusalem by the scribes and Pharisees, stoned and had his head caved in by a fuller's club!

But James the Less is one of those Jesus was referring to when he prayed to the father "they are not of the world any more than I am of the world", and he was among those to whom Jesus said *"go into all the world"*[240]. He is every bit as much an apostle as Peter, James and John, and just as loved by and valuable to God.

This is important in today's culture because all too frequently our heads are turned by how many likes our shares our social media posts accrue, how many followers our twitter feed has or how many facebook friends we have.

Jesus says to us plainly: ultimately, that stuff is worthless. He says don't do things to be seen by men, but understand that God sees the things you do when you're on your own, and he sees the thoughts in your heart that you don't reveal to anyone.

In fact Jesus says that if that is our motivation, when men notice and applaud us for that stuff, the reward has already come. Jesus says our Father rewards those things which honour Him which we do in secret.

It has been said that if you live for the praise of men, then their criticism will kill you.

Eternity will reveal the names and testimonies of people who, like James are barely noticed or remembered in this world. We do not need to seek fame and notoriety in this life to have significance in the kingdom of God. God sees us even when we're completely invisible to the world.

AND in fact, God sees us even if we're completely invisible in the church as well.

We can expect him to touch us, to give us his gifts and fill us with his spirit every bit as much as the most famous Christian you have ever heard of. Our value comes not from men, but from our Father who is in heaven

James the Less teaches us powerfully that we can walk unnoticed and practically invisible through life, that even if we're never given an accolade by men, or even those around us, every one of us can still fulfil his purpose for our life. And on the day we stand before God, we will receive the ultimate accolade: *"well done, Good and faithful servant, you have been faithful. Come and share your master's happiness"*[241].

The following is one of the passages which most encourages me when I feel invisible or unnoticed and disregarded: *"Brothers, think of what you were when you were called. Not many of you were wise by human standards; not many were influential; not many were of noble birth. But God chose the foolish things of the world to shame the wise; God chose the weak things of the world to shame the strong. He chose the lowly things of this world and the despised things–and the things that are not - to nullify the things that are, so that no one may boast before him. It is because of him that you are in Christ Jesus, who has become for us wisdom from God–that is, our righteousness, holiness and redemption. Therefore, as it is written:"Let him who boasts boast in the Lord"*[242].

Paul lists here some traits that describe some ways in which we might be "not people" and I've given some Biblical examples of such people God used to help us to get a handle on this issue.

Not wise(26) but foolish(27) i.e. Mental Attributes

The first category is that of mental ability, people who are or feel somehow that they fall short. Paul describes human "wisdom" as foolishness. I want to extend that slightly to include some other areas internally.

Moses couldn't find the words he needed (he knows it and says so at the burning bush)

The disciples were *"ordinary, unschooled men"*[243].

It is interesting that Paul was someone whose schooling was reckoned to be one of the best of his time. He says *"Under Gamaliel I was thoroughly trained in the law of our fathers"*[244], yet he also says, *"I may not be a trained speaker, but I do have knowledge"*[245]

I meet many people who feel inadequate because they didn't do well at school, they feel that somehow things they did (or rather didn't) do at school prevents them from being effective for God. There is a tendency nowadays to equate education with intelligence.

But wisdom and foolishness isn't just about education, it's also about other forms of mental strength and ability, or lack of it:

1. Jacob was a liar. Even his name means "he deceives"[246].
2. Joseph was spoiled. Remember his attitude to his brothers?[247] (actually, apart from Benjamin, they were his half brothers).
3. James & John had tempers [248]

4. Peter was impulsive (foot in mouth disease)
5. Gideon had real issues with fear (a coward?) and had very little faith
6. We live with a sense of inferiority and far too often compare ourselves with one another: "I'm not as good as him or her". We play the comparison game so well don't we? Even Peter did it, he looked at John and said *"master what about him?"* Jesus' response was, *"what's that to you? YOU follow me"*[249].

Sometimes our own inner weaknesses make us vulnerable to things which are not good. I have a friend who is very open in his testimony about his alcoholism, and by his own admission he was on the fast track to an early grave. But he found Christ and became a "new creation", so that is now his past! It died on the cross with Christ and in NO WAY excludes him from being used in the kingdom of God. How about the rest of us? Do we have a tendency to something we're ashamed of: porn? Smoking? Gossip? Quick temper? Being negative?

Do you feel that there is something inside which means you are hesitant about going for God? Something which you feel somehow disqualifies you from service in His church, or on the mission field?

Strength: weak (v27)

Ehud was left-handed[250]

Abraham was old and childless. Genesis 12:4 tells us he was 75 when he set out from Haran.

It is thought that Paul had some kind of physical infirmity (his *"thorn in the flesh"*[251]). So often in our churches, people feel that they don't qualify because of some physical issue.

Sometimes people feel they are too old, saying things like: "my time is past" or "it's time to pass the baton on". This denies the obvious times God called older people to do His work, it also denies the passion of older people, Caleb was 80 and one of the most passionate of his day. A very good Christian friend of mine Tony Lee was 78 when he and I went on mission to Uganda!

In contrast, others see themselves as too young. The other end of the spectrum denies ministry to the young because they are too young, although we often don't say that, we say they "need more life experience". I have taken young people as young as 12 & 13 on mission, and in fact our own children were VERY small (pre-school age) when we started taking them on mission.

Don't buy into this clap-trap that age is a factor that contributes to whether God uses you or not! Abraham was 75, David was about 13 (but nearly 40 before he actually became king), Josiah was 8 when he became king, Moses was about 80 when God called him. When they were called, the disciples' ages could have been anything in the range from mid-teens to early 40's, Paul wrote to Timothy *"don't let anyone look down on you because you are young"*[252], John was elderly when God gave him the vision of heaven that we know as Revelation. So Whether you are just starting out in life, or in what we might call your golden years, don't buy the lie that your usefulness for God is determined by your age!

Your weakness could be a physical disability. But that need not stop you. One of the most memorable worship leaders I have ever known was blind, an awesome keyboard player, and SO used by God to lead worship. Think also about people like Kathryn Kuhlman, Joni Erickson (insert your own examples here). You may have crutches or some form of medical device to help you live life, but don't believe for one minute that it will stop God's call on you.

Perhaps it's a combination of age and disability, some infirmity which is coming on as you are getting older (arthritis for example). Many people struggle with some kind of infirmity, which they think relegates them to the sidelines and watching other people do great things and have great adventures for the Lord.

Please hear me I am NOT saying the struggles you have (either physically or emotionally) are not real or that you just have to somehow muster enough faith to say "that's it, I'm not putting up with such and such any more", or that if you struggle with your weakness then you are somehow not "living in victory brother". What I am saying is don't let it define you, don't write yourself out of God's plan for your church, your town, your area because of it. God has a plan for your life and he can use you in your weakness. You STILL have a part to play and you are still immeasurably valuable to God, just give him it all.

Nobility / birthright / privilege: "not of noble birth" (v26)

When you look at people in the Christian world, it is noticeable how many well-known Christin leaders have children who have followed them into ministry, and you could be forgiven for thinking that it's as much about who your family are as it is about your calling.

Don't misunderstand me, I'm not saying that any of the preacher's / leader's kids we might name etc are not gifted or called by God, or that they don't deserve to be in the ministries they have. What I AM saying is, don't look at those people and assume that because you don't come from the "right" family like they do that God won't use you!

Gideon was the "least" in the smallest family in the smallest tribe[253].

Jephthah, was a half brother in his family (and by a prostitute) he was driven away by his half brothers and told he had no place in the family and would have no part in the inheritance[254]. Yet God used him.

Jesus was from Nazareth and Nathanael asked *"can anything good come from there?"*[255]. Our place of origin affects how we see ourselves, and in the UK at least, different areas have different subcultures which may prove a barrier to our ministering effectively in them.

There may be something in your past or family environment which you feel has disqualified you in some way from His service. So many people live with the belief that we should have had the same experience as other we know who are serving God and because we haven't it clearly means we're not as gifted / skilled / called or whatever as them.

We do not nowadays, by and large, have class privilege, but there is no doubt that other factors also influence our sense of self-worth. Certainly location is a big thing. If you live in an affluent suburb, and were to say to someone in some council tenement in a deprived inner city that we all have equal opportunities, you would probably get mugged!

It is sad to say that actually I have watched the growth of what I would call "reverse snobbery" going on in our society. I have witnessed people who are perceived as being privileged (he/she was born with a silver spoon in their mouth) being overlooked for roles, especially in more deprived areas.

This includes things we grew up doing and things that are not so historic.

Value: lowly & despised (v27)

So often, what others think of us or say about us can stop us moving into the victory God has for us! In

Judges 6:27-32 we already know that Gideon cut down the Asherah pole (at night), and was rejected by the people, in fact only his father's intervention saved him. Joshua 2:1 tells us that Rahab was a prostitute (and by implication, morally corrupt by her own actions), yet she was used by God mightily.

In the Parable of the prodigal son[256], the son was morally and financially bankrupt. I know he isn't a real person, but the parable shows how God views us when we come to him from the pigs!

Matthew (Levi) was a tax collector[257]. Tax Collectors were hated so much they weren't lumped in with "sinners", but had their very own category of being hated!

The man born blind in John 9 was invisible to people around him. No one could even agree who he was when he was healed. Isaiah 53:2 is a description of the suffering servant and a prophecy concerning Jesus. It says of him: *"He had no beauty or majesty to attract us to him, nothing in his appearance that we should desire him"*.

People may criticise us, our character, our skills, our gifting, and if it has come from someone we love or look up to it can completely hamstring us. When I was 14 I was told I couldn't sing, had no musical ability at all and not to bother choosing music for my exams. It stopped me getting involved in music and worship until I was in my mid 40s. I now lead worship regularly and have taught guitar and worship at a Seminary in India.

Jackie Pullinger, George Whitefield, Hudson Taylor, Smith Wigglesworth, William Carey, and many others were all rejected for service in the church or on the mission field, yet they all went on to do great things for God.

Hope for Us...

I want us to notice that, firstly, Paul invites us to think about ourselves here. The passage lists some things we can consider, but it also gives us the WHY this is such an important thing to grasp.

Think of what you were, Paul says. Understand yourself, and understand what it is that God chooses, the type of people HE esteems. The type of people He calls. Ultimately it is God's sovereign choice which defines our value, not our personal characteristics, whatever they are. The Good News for us is that God doesn't listen to the opinions of others. God doesn't look at our pedigree, our past performance, take references, or give probationary periods before deciding whether or not you are useful to Him in the Kingdom and confirming your appointment as his ambassador!

So the whole point of what Paul is saying here is that one of the reasons God deliberately seems to choose unknown, invisible, flawed people is **So that we don't think it is us who has done it.!**

Gideon's army is whittled down from 33,000 to just 300, and listen to God's description as to WHY: *"The LORD said to Gideon, "You have too many men. I cannot* deliver Midian into their hands, or Israel would boast against me, 'My own strength has saved me.'"[258].

In other words, we have a tendency to think that we can do the things God has called us to do. God told Abraham he would be a father of nations, but his wife Sarah was too old to bear children. Abraham tried to give God a helping hand by having a child with her maidservant, Hagar (and that didn't that turn out well at all).

Flawed people often know who they are.

Paul reminds the Corinthians who they were. He points out their flaws, he points out that they didn't exhibit any of the characteristics of people who would normally be viewed by the world as the right type. And that is EXACTLY why they are chosen.

God's track record is one of choosing things that are not and making them into something[259]. He chose a nation before it was even born, he chose prophets before they were born.

Jeremiah is told, *"Before I formed you in the womb I knew (or chose) you, before you were born I set you apart"*[260].

Isaiah knew that *"Before I was born, the Lord called me; from my birth he has made mention of my name"*[261].

God knows what we were like: *"Do you not know that the wicked will not inherit the kingdom of God? Do not be deceived: Neither the sexually immoral nor idolaters nor adulterers nor male prostitutes nor homosexual offenders nor thieves nor the greedy nor drunkards nor slanderers nor swindlers will inherit the kingdom of God. And that is what some of you were. But you were washed, you were sanctified,* you were justified in the name of the Lord Jesus Christ and by the Spirit of our God"262.

He chose you and I when we were dead in our sin: "As for you, you were dead in your transgressions and sins, in which you used to live when you followed the ways of this world and of the ruler of the kingdom of the air, the spirit who is now at work in those who are disobedient. All of us also lived among them at one time, gratifying the cravings of our sinful nature and following its desires and thoughts. Like the rest, we were by nature objects of wrath"263.

He makes something of us and calls us to things we never believed possible, "God who gives life to the dead and calls things that are not as though they were"264.

God has chosen the way of weakness, "Has not God chosen those who are poor in the eyes of the world to be rich in faith and to inherit the kingdom he promised those who love him?"265.

The ultimate hope for us, though, is this: "Think of yourselves the way Christ Jesus thought of himself. He had equal status with God but didn't think so much of himself that he had to cling to the advantages of that status no matter what. Not at all. When the time came, he set aside the privileges of deity and took on the status of a slave, became human! Having become human, he stayed human. It was an incredibly humbling process. He didn't claim special privileges. Instead, he lived a selfless, obedient life and then died a selfless, obedient death—and the worst kind of death at that:a crucifixion"266.

In a very real way Jesus, though he was a something, became a someone who "was not", and it was in that action that we have the most significant life in human history.

Don't believe the lie that the "not" of your life disqualifies you from anything God might call you to do. Your mission / function is not dependent on you, your past, your skills and gifting, it is entirely up to The Lord whom He chooses. Whatever you are carrying which you think is a block to the power of God working through you is something that God is aware of yet he chooses you anyway!

If you remember nothing else from James the Less, remember this. Often God doesn't choose us despite our flaws, he often chooses us BECAUSE of them!

10. Simon the Zealot

How would you like to be called Dave the terrorist? Or Susan the murderer? That is exactly how Simon is described. Zealots were a group of Jews who believed that Rome had no place in Israel and that the only way to remove them is through force and insurrection. They had no hesitation killing any Roman they could and those who collaborated with them.

What can we learn from this domestic terrorist?

Passion - go for it!

Look up "definition of Zealous" on Google and you will be told it is an "(adjective) marked by fervent partisanship for a person, a cause, or an ideal : filled with or characterised by zeal". I wish that every Christian I meet would be a Zealot according to that definition!

For the Zealots of Jesus's day, this passion and zeal spilled over into physical action and violence towards those who opposed them. The challenge for us is to retain the passion and zeal without allowing it to spill over into violence.

A few weeks ago, on one of my daily dog walking exercises, I met a couple also out for a walk. During the course of our conversation, the subject of my ministry came up. On realising I was a local church leader, they wanted to know what the church was like. This is quite common, as is the question the man asked: "yours isn't one of those "happy clappy" churches, is it?" The embedded implication which is particularly strong in British culture is a mistrust of people who are passionate about something, especially if it involves some form of emotionalism (unless it's support of a sports team).

It never ceases to amaze me that no one bats an eye if thousands of men jump and shout and scream and cheer when a man kicks a bag of wind into a net strung between two posts without being criticised (I'm talking about soccer of course), but if I show a degree of passion when worshipping the King of kings and Lord of lords, I am dismissed as being overly emotional and somehow not quite British!

But the Bible commends zeal, Jesus is recorded by the Gospels as saying, *"Love the Lord your God with **ALL** your heart and with **ALL** your soul and with **ALL** your strength and with **ALL** your mind'; and, 'Love your neighbour as yourself"*[267]. Paul writes *"Never be lacking in zeal, but keep your **spiritual fervour**, serving the Lord"*[268]. He also says, *"Whatever you do, work at it with **all your heart**, as working for the Lord, not for human masters"*[269], these verses (among others) show us not only the importance of wholehearted commitment, they also tell us why …

"Love the Lord"

"Serving the Lord"

"Working for the Lord"

See the common thread? Everything we do, the effort we put into our lives, is all for The Lord. Who we are, how we act, is fundamentally determined for us by our faith. It is, however, possible to lose our zeal. It happened to the Ephesians, and Jesus says what he thinks about it: *"Yet I hold this against you: You have forsaken the love you had at first"*[270]. Lack of zeal is also something that happened to the Laodicean church: *"I know your deeds, that you are neither cold nor hot. I wish you were either one or the other! So, because you are lukewarm — neither hot nor cold — I am about to spit you out of my mouth"*[271].

God says *"These people honour me with their lips, but their hearts are far from me"*[272].

This is the first thing Simon the Zealot teaches us, we must never lose our passion for God, we must follow through with our actions, but those actions must not spill over into violence.

Hatred - Love your enemies

Secondly, Jesus also chose Matthew as a disciple, a man who was a tax-collector and collaborator (and by implication an enemy to Simon). All his life, Simon would have been taught about and encouraged to give expression to his hatred in violence towards his enemies. The teachings of Jesus about loving and forgiving one's enemy, and that inner hatred for someone being poisonous, must have been a real challenge when someone he would have viewed as an enemy was living in such close proximity.

But a life spent in hatred is no life at all. It has been said that hatred is like a cancer which feeds on its host. It is a madness in the spirit which quenches all pity and corrupts all judgement. It distorts our view of others. Hatred is a spiritual disease. Like unforgiveness, hatred damages the hater far more than the hated, and Simon was part of a group which fed off hatred.

Why did Simon initially follow Jesus? The gospels don't answer this question, but in following Jesus, Simon would have soon learned that hatred has no place in the hearts of those who do. Jesus taught a different way, he taught that we should love our enemies, that we should do good to those who hate us[273]. Paul picks up on this in Romans 12:20 when he quotes Proverbs 25:21: *"If your enemy is hungry, feed him; if he is thirsty, give him something to drink"*. The Proverbs verse is significant because it shows us that the concept of loving rather than killing your enemy is something that is not a new idea introduced by Jesus, it is part of the very nature of God.

It is not without reason that in one of the most well-known parables Jesus teaches, it is a Samaritan who showed he was a good neighbour. Samaritans and Jews were enemies, the history between them stretched back centuries. The armies of Samaria and their leader Sanballat the Horonite had opposed Nehemiah 500 years before when he rebuilt the wall of Jerusalem[274], history had grown an almost irreconcilable difference between Jews and Samaritans[275]. The impact Jesus made in referencing a Samaritan as a good neighbour cannot be overstated, and its implications about loving one's enemies should not be overlooked.

Jesus calls his followers to love their enemies, he also talks about how we should relate to them. In the larger passage in Luke which is all about loving our enemies[276], he says in Luke 6:35 *"love your enemies, do good to them, and lend to them without expecting to get anything back"*. Matthew picks up on this in Matthew 5:43-48 and says much the same.

Jesus modelled this radical love even in the face of vitriolic hate, he showed us that love for our enemies trumps everything else — even to the point of going to the cross for them. This radical love, Paul says, is exactly what reconciled God's enemies to him: *"For if, while we were God's enemies, we were reconciled to him through the death of his Son, how much more, having been reconciled, shall we be saved through his life!"*[277].

If we are truly to be followers of Jesus, we must love our enemies.

Hatred - Forgive those who hate you

Simon's attitude towards the Romans, his background of hatred and violence towards his enemy, had to give way to one of forgiveness and grace and going the extra mile. Forgiveness is frequently the gateway to loving one's enemies. It is difficult, if not impossible, to love someone you cannot forgive.

Simon the Zealot was a disciple alongside Matthew the Tax Collector - two enemies who were gathered by Jesus into a group who were called to be friends. Jesus calls us to turn our enemies into friends, he calls us to forgive, to leave our old lives behind and follow the new way of Christ.

In September 1988 there was a news report about a man whose son had been killed by a drunk driver who fled the scene. With no evidence the police had been unable to bring charges. The father had spent years watching and recording the man who escaped justice, gathering evidence, and finally getting to the place where he was able to help the police gain a conviction. Justice had prevailed. Yet in the unfolding of the story, the overwhelming sense was that his obsession and desire for revenge had trapped him.

About that same time I remember the killing of a young black man by thugs in central London. A horrific attack motivated by hate and racism. His parents were interviewed, and when asked what they thought of the men who had been convicted of the crime, they expressed and offered forgiveness towards the attackers. The astounded interviewer asked why didn't they hate them, and their response was one which I will never forget, "don't you think there's enough hate in the world already?"

Which of these parents do you think was more free?

Forgiveness is foundational to the Christian faith. It is at the heart of the cross, and it should be at the heart of our relationships with each other. It is one of the paths to freedom and one of the key ingredients to our fellowship one with another. Paul calls us to *"bear with each other and forgive one another if any of you has a grievance against someone. Forgive as the Lord forgave you"*[278], and to *"be kind and compassionate to one another, forgiving each other, just as in Christ God forgave you"*[279].

The Lord's prayer, one of the foundational prayers in the Christian faith, recognises the importance of forgiveness: *"forgive our trespasses as we forgive those who trespass against us"*. Jesus goes on to say that if we do not forgive others their sins against us, neither will our Father in heaven forgive us our sins[280].

Do not underestimate the importance or power of forgiveness, and note that nowhere in the Bible do we find qualifications on this. When someone hurts us, we are to forgive them, whether or not they have asked for it.

So, for example, some years ago we had an experience where some people we thought were friends said and did some things which hurt us very deeply. They were not repentant when told about it. In fact they justified their words and actions asserting that given the same circumstances they would say and do exactly the same things again - the issue they said was ours and not theirs. This personal experience has taught me that it is possible for someone to not only hurt you, but to show no remorse at all, and that Jesus does not give us a let-out on forgiveness. There are no "ifs" or exclusions to His command to forgive. Forgiveness is to be extended even to our enemies. Our calling and responsibility is to unilaterally offer and give forgiveness wherever we have been hurt. Unforgiveness has been described as drinking poison and hoping the other person will die. Unforgiveness damages ME and not the other person.

I'll leave you with the words of Jesus: *"love your enemies, do good to them, and lend to them without expecting to get anything back. Then your reward will be great, and you will be children of the Most High, because he is kind to the ungrateful and wicked. Be merciful, just as your Father is merciful"*[281].

If you do that you will escape hate which will imprison you, dominate your life and consume you from the inside out.

11. Thaddaeus (Judas, son of James)

This disciple is identified as Judas (not Iscariot) by John, as Judas son of James by Luke, and as Thaddaeus by Matthew and Mark. (The King James Bible also uses the name Lebbaeus in Matthew 10:3, though in other translations his name in this verse is Thaddaeus. I've looked, and according to my Greek New Testament, the correct translation here is Thaddaeus, so I believe the NIV, ESV and other translations are more accurate. Exactly WHY this discrepancy in the translations arises, I don't know, but this is not the place to go into the discipline of textual criticism).

For the purposes of this chapter unless I am directly quoting scripture, I will refer to "Judas not Iscariot, the son of James" as Thaddaeus.

Thaddaeus

The first thing I want to do is spend a few moments on this name, Thaddaeus.

You may remember that earlier when looking at James and John, I looked at Jesus naming them Boanerges because of their hot tempers, and noted the custom of naming people according to their attributes. So as well as the example of James and John, we have the encourager Joseph of Cyprus being called Barnabas (meaning son of encouragement), and most notably, Simon was called Cephas (Peter in English) by Jesus which means rock. Since using names with meaning was not unusual, it is at least possible that calling Judas by the name "Thaddaeus" was not a mistake.

But why call him Thaddaeus? There are several possibilities: Thaddaeus may have been a family nickname he used. It might have been a name given to him by the other disciples or even by Jesus. How he came to be called Thaddaeus we just don't know, the Bible is silent on this matter. What we do know is that the name Thaddaeus in Hebrew literally means "breast child", and the Gospels use it to identify him, and if the custom of naming people because of some attribute they had holds true for Thaddaeus just as it did for James, John and Simon Peter, this is significant. John MacArthur suggests in his book[282] that it may have a meaning similar to our term "mummy's boy", but we cannot be sure whether that was the reason or not.

What I do believe is that the name Thaddaeus speaks to his heart nature, to the man he was, to his character. Even the name Lebbaeus which as I've said is used by the KJV has a similar meaning "heart child". I suspect that Thaddaeus was a gentle man, one with a tenderness in his heart towards God, towards Jesus, and indeed towards his fellow man. I believe this is revealed in his question, which we will turn to later on.

I think this is important because Jesus is clear (in fact the Bible repeatedly asserts) that it is in our heart that our true nature lies. So if you want to know the true nature of a man, you don't look primarily at his actions, you look at his heart. Jesus says it is what is in a man's heart that dictates his actions and in the sermon on the mount[283] He says that the heart determines the sin, so:

1. Lust in the heart IS adultery.
2. Anger in the heart IS murder.

And so on. Jesus says elsewhere that it is not what goes into a man which makes him unclean, but what comes out of his heart. So for example

"Are you still so dull?" Jesus asked them. "Don't you see that whatever enters the mouth goes into the stomach and then out of the body? But the things that come out of a person's mouth **come from the heart***, and these defile them. For out of the heart come evil thoughts—murder, adultery, sexual immorality, theft, false testimony, slander. These are what defile a person; but eating with unwashed hands does not defile them."*[284]

The key to our being right with God lies not in our actions, but in our hearts, which is why the promise of God is not that he will make us do good things, but rather that he will change our hearts:

Ezekiel prophesies it twice. Ezekiel 11:19 says *"I will give them an undivided heart and put a new spirit in them; I will remove from them their heart of stone and give them a heart of flesh"*, and Ezekiel 36:26 says *"I will give you a new heart and put a new spirit in you; I will remove from you your heart of stone and give you a heart of flesh"*.

God says to Jeremiah: *"I will give them a heart to know me, that I am the LORD. They will be my people, and I will be their God, for they will return to me with all their heart"*[285]. Paul alludes to this change in 2 Corinthians 5:17 when he says, *"Therefore, if anyone is in Christ, the new creation has come: The old has gone, the new is here!"*

So, Christ comes not to change our actions, but to renew our hearts and Spirits. When our hearts are changed, we have a new nature, and consequently, our actions follow. So for example, Ezekiel follows his prophecy about God giving a new heart with this promise about what will happen when we are transformed by him: *"And I will put my Spirit in you and move you to follow my decrees and be careful to keep my laws. Then you will live in the land I gave your ancestors; you will be my people, and I will be your God"*[286].

We often miss this, and I frequently find people seeing faith in Christ and the role of the Church as a mechanism for controlling what we do, not changing what we are. This belief couldn't be more of a misunderstanding of who Jesus is and what he came to do if it tried. It reaches right back to Biblical times, and even then, people thought holiness was primarily a matter of keeping the law, and not a matter of the heart. It was about what you did and not who you were.

In Acts 2 Peter preaches to the people, Luke records the reaction as *"they were cut to the heart"*, yet they thought they had to DO something *"brothers what shall we **do**?"*[287].

Interestingly, people ask Jesus on numerous occasions what they should DO to inherit eternal life, and on one occasion he is asked *"What must we do to do the works God requires?"* His response is: *"The work of God is this: to believe in the one he has sent"* [288]. Paul talks of belief being a characteristic of the HEART and not the intellect ... *"If you declare with your mouth, "Jesus is Lord," and believe in your heart that God raised him from the dead, you will be saved. For it is with your heart that you believe and are justified, and it is with your mouth that you profess your faith and are saved"*[289].

This is ultimately why Christians are not (or should not be) in the business of imposing rules and restrictions on people's actions, but in the business of offering them a change of heart, a change of their very nature from enemy of God to his friend.

And, counter-intuitively, when we do that, our actions follow our beliefs in any event and we live the life and do the things which God requires anyway...

"He has shown you, O man, what is good.
And what does the LORD require of you?
To act justly and to love mercy
and to walk humbly with your God"[290].

Even here note, three things:

1. Action (Act Justly),
2. Heart (love mercy) and
3. Faith (walk humbly with your God).

Neglect any one of those and you are not living up to the requirement God himself has laid down.

The Question

These are the only recorded words of Thaddaeus:

"Then Judas (not Judas Iscariot) said, "But, Lord, why do you intend to show yourself to us and not to the world?"[291]

It does put me in mind of a very common objection to the message of the Gospel, which is: "what about people who have never heard?" This question is usually disingenuous in the sense that all too frequently it is asked not because the questioner genuinely wants an answer, but because he or she wants to justify rejecting the Gospel.

Thaddaeus is not doing that, he is articulating a common belief among the Jews of his day that the Messiah would be a recognised, national figure who would bring his people back to freedom and restore the nation as a force to be reckoned with in the world, and why, if He is the Messiah, doesn't he act in the way they expected?

> *Aside: I am sure I am not unique in this: over the years I've dreamed about the future or mulled over a particular situation, and pondered about what God would do in it. "Wouldn't it be great if God did (such and*

such) for us?" Rarely, if ever, did things work out the way I'd dreamed. This is very similar in nature to the expectation of the Jews about what the Messiah would be like.

God rarely works to our expectations. In Isaiah, he says: *"As the heavens are higher than the earth, so are my ways higher than your ways and my thoughts than your thoughts"*[292].

The writer of Proverbs tells us that *"There is a way that appears to be right, but in the end it leads to death"*[293], and *"In their hearts humans plan their course, but the LORD establishes their steps"*[294].

Jesus didn't come to bring political freedom to the Jews, he didn't come to overthrow the Roman occupation, he came to release people from the slavery of sin. He was never going to come as a national leader in a large, visible way. His life and ministry showed that again and again. He even withdrew at one point because he knew people wanted to come and make him king by force[295]. This is a lesson to us about predicting how God will work in our lives or the lives of those around us, otherwise we may find ourselves saying to him, "why did you do it that way?"

So let's unpack the question, which is like a coin with two sides:

1. Why us? (i.e. what make me so special?)
2. Why not them? (i.e. don't they deserve to know as well?)

Why us?

Hebrews 2:6 says *"What is man that you are mindful of him the son of man that you care for him?"*[296].

"Why me, Lord?" We often say this when something happens to us which is unpleasant or unexpected, but Nathanael isn't saying it in this sense. He is saying, "what makes us so special?". We live in a culture which is preoccupied with self-esteem. Sometimes it seems that people believe that a healthy self-esteem is the answer to all of life's problems, that if we can somehow change the way we think about ourselves, start seeing ourselves positively and stop thinking negatively, then all our problems will suddenly disappear. Yet, we also have a deep-rooted mistrust of people who have no humility. We use expressions like "he thinks he's God's gift", or "He's too big for his boots" to express how we feel about such people. If someone's assessment of you is "You think you're too good for me", you will find it hard, if not impossible, to say anything meaningful into their life.

There was an attitude which the Pharisees had that mirrored this, Jesus tells a parable which we are told was aimed at those who *"were confident of their own righteousness and looked down on everyone else"*[297]. This was not seen as a good thing. In fact, Jesus goes on to say that when you compare such a person with one who kneels before God in humility, that it is the humble man and not the confident one who is deemed justified. This parable actually answers the question, "why us?" It says that those who ask "who am I" are exactly the people God will reveal himself to. That is, those who do not have too high an opinion of themselves. *"For all those who exalt themselves will be humbled, and those who humble themselves will be exalted"*[298].

Paul writes *"do not think more highly of yourself than you ought"*[299], rather our attitude should be the same as that of Jesus who Paul says *"being in very nature God, did not consider equality with God something to be used to his own advantage; rather, he made himself nothing by taking the very nature of a servant, being made in human likeness. And being found in appearance as a man, he humbled himself by becoming obedient to death — even death on a cross"* [300].

Isaiah says *"This is the one I esteem: he who is humble and contrite in spirit, and trembles at my word"*[301], and *"For this is what the high and exalted One says — he who lives forever, whose name is holy: "I live in a high and holy place, but also with the one who is contrite and lowly in spirit"*[302]

Thaddaeus's question revealed that he was just such a man, it showed that his heart is one which God esteems. The one who is lowly and contrite of heart, and who just can't quite believe that Jesus would come to him and not someone else. The question itself is the answer.

Jesus could have answered: *because you asked the question "why me?"*

Why not them?

The answer to the question "why not them?" is obvious if we think about it. Spiritual sight is, unsurprisingly, something which is not a characteristic of the unspiritual man.

1 Corinthians 2:14 says this bluntly: *"The person without the Spirit does not accept the things that come from the Spirit of God, but considers them foolishness, and cannot understand them because they are discerned only through the Spirit".*

Thaddaeus is responding to Jesus' teaching on the Holy Spirit, and Jesus has just made these comments:

1. *"The world cannot accept the Holy Spirit because it neither sees Him nor knows him"*[303].
2. *"In a short while, the world will not see me* (Jesus) *any more"* [304] (this is a hint about the crucifixion).

It is interesting that Paul declares in Romans, God IS visible in creation, and if we will just look we will find him there. In fact if we can't, the fault is ours.

*"For since the creation of the world God's invisible qualities—his eternal power and divine nature—have been clearly seen, being understood from what has been made, **so that people are without excuse**"*[305].

The reason we are told that people don't see God is that *"the god of this age has blinded the minds of unbelievers, so that they cannot see the light of the gospel that displays the glory of Christ, who is the image of God"*[306].

"He was not seen by all the people, but by witnesses whom God had already chosen—by us who ate and drank with him after he rose from the dead. He commanded us to preach to the people and to testify that he is the one whom God appointed as judge of the living and the dead"[307].

John 14:23 is Jesus' answer to Thaddaeus' question: *"Jesus replied, "Anyone who loves me will obey my teaching. My Father will love them, and we will come to them and make our home with them"*. Jesus explains that seeing God, having Jesus revealed, is a pretty simple thing. Anyone, he says, and obeys his teaching can see him.

Given that the world neither loves Jesus nor obeys his teaching, and that the world is blind to Him, shows us that the blindness of the world about him is largely self-inflicted. Many people will say "I won't believe unless you can show me Jesus", but Jesus says "you won't see me unless you believe", and your belief is characterised by, and seen in, your obedience.

And finally ...

This is implied by though not explicitly revealed in the text there will come a time when Jesus returns, and that time it will not be missed! *"Look, he is coming with the clouds,"* and *"every eye will see him,*
even those who pierced him"; and all peoples on earth "will mourn because of him." So shall it be! Amen"[308].

Matthew 24:26,27 says *"if anyone tells you, 'There he is, out in the wilderness,' do not go out; or, 'Here he is, in the* inner rooms,' do not believe it. For as lightning that comes from the east is visible even in the west, so will be the coming of the Son of Man", and he goes on to describe that "at that time the sign of the Son of Man will appear in the sky, and all the nations of the earth will mourn. They will see the Son of Man coming on the clouds of the sky, with power and great glory".

This event is spoken of in great detail in Revelation 19:11-16, "I saw heaven standing open and there before me was a white horse, whose rider is called Faithful and True. With justice, he judges and makes war. His eyes are like blazing fire, and on his head are many crowns. He has a name written on him that no one knows but he himself. He is dressed in a robe dipped in blood, and his name is the Word of God. The armies of heaven were following him, riding on white horses and dressed in fine linen, white and clean. Out of his mouth comes a sharp sword with which to strike down the nations. "He will rule them with an iron sceptre." He treads the winepress of the fury of the wrath of God Almighty. On his robe and on his thigh he has this name written: KING OF KINGS AND LORD OF LORDS."

Titus 2:13 describes the second coming as a "glorious appearing."

He will one day reveal his glory to the whole world!

12. Judas Iscariot

In Jesus' time, being called Judas was a GOOD thing! Judas is the Greek form of the Hebrew personal name Judah meaning, "Praise Yahweh", and was quite a common name.

Judas Iscariot is placed by all of the Gospel writers at the end of the list of disciples because of the part he played in the arrest of Jesus. Judas is nothing like the man Julian Lloyd Webber portrays in the musical Jesus Christ superstar (which I love, by the way).

Iscariot is an Aramaic word which means "man of Kerioth", which is a town near Hebron. He was the only disciple from Judea. He acted as treasurer for the disciples but was known as a miser and a thief, so for example when Jesus was anointed at Bethany, it is Judas who says *"Why wasn't this perfume sold and the money given to the poor? It was worth a year's wages"* And John's assessment is that *"he did not say this because he cared about the poor but because he was a thief; as keeper of the money bag, he used to help himself to what was put into it"*[309].

Ultimately though, what Judas is remembered for is not the fact he was a thief, but that he betrayed Jesus, so much so that in our unchristian secular culture, the name Judas has become such a negative term that it has all but ceased being a name at all. I don't know of anyone called Judas today, and I don't know anyone who would call their son Judas. So I searched that fount of all knowledge, Google for stats on how many people have been named Judas and found that in the USA, in 2018 (the last year for which I could find figures for the name) of the 3 million births that year, only 17 were named Judas.

So, what can we learn today from this disciple who is pretty much universally regarded with repulsion?

Proximity to Jesus will not necessarily give you immunity from Sin.

"Going to church does not make you a Christian, any more than going to MacDonalds makes you a hamburger!" We all know that being in Church is not what makes us Christians. We go to church because we are Christians, we are not Christians because we go to church! But this points to something deeper than that. Some people regard Jesus or their faith in Him as some kind of charm or talisman against sin. All I have to do to keep from sinning, they contend, is to stay as close as I can to the Lord and I won't sin. Well the story of Judas teaches that this is not necessarily the case, Judas sinned. Judas spent 3 years as one of Jesus' disciples, he lived among the disciples, WITH Jesus. He was with him every day, he saw the miracles, he heard and listened to the teaching, yet he still sinned. He still let the Lord down.

Jesus himself alludes to this, he says, *"why do you call me Lord, Lord? And don't do what I say?"*[310].

We also read in Hosea 8:2ff._ "Israel cries out to me, 'O our God, we acknowledge you! 'But Israel has rejected what is good"_, and then Hosea spells out what that looks like: Just saying I love you God and not living it is called "lip service" in the Bible and it is worthless.

It is important to understand though that It was not only Judas who failed, Peter denied him, Thomas didn't believe he was risen, all of the disciples ran away and hid. In one way or another they all misunderstood and fell away even though they spent time in Jesus company.

Why do we Fall into Sin?

So, why sometimes, despite our proximity to Jesus, do we do things which we know are not His wish for us?

We Choose To

Often people sin because they choose to. We might point to all sorts of reasons why we sin, but in the end, it all boils down to choice, far too frequently sin is in our lives because we are not willing to remove it.

We read of Judas that he was a thief and the keeper of the disciples' purse. That he kept the purse may not have been a choice for him, but that he was a thief was entirely under his control. Too commonly nowadays we have a culture in which people will avoid responsibility for every action, they will make all sorts of excuses to justify even the abhorrent things they do. People rioted in the summer, they burnt and looted shops, they destroyed property, they engaged in all sorts of antisocial behaviour and some people on the media were not only refusing to condemn the violence and law-breaking, they were condoning it. Why? Because people were angry, they said. But every single person in every single riot, whether in Bristol or Washington or anywhere else, made a choice. Every single person in the rioting crowd made a choice to break the law.

Even in churches, where the right choice should be obvious, people choose to disobey God. Sadly all too often in our churches we see people who are not living as the Bible teaches, some don't bother to hide it and occasionally you find people are even proud of themselves in it, but this is not always the case. More frequently people who have deliberate sin in their lives look exactly like everyone else, they try hide their sin, so for example, there have been a couple of high-profile Christian leaders in the last couple of years who have accommodated and even pursued sinful behaviour despite preaching the way of Christ. I won't name them, but it seems to me that with frightening regularity one person or another fails because some hidden sin has been uncovered. The damage to the Gospel in such instances is saddening, and the church, far from being salt and light, becomes like the culture it is supposed to challenge.

Paul speaks about this kind of person in Romans 1. He says this *"they did not think it worthwhile to retain the knowledge of God, so God gave them over to a depraved mind, so that they do what ought not to be done. They have become filled with every kind of wickedness, evil, greed and depravity. They are full of envy, murder, strife, deceit and malice. They are gossips, slanderers, God-haters, insolent, arrogant and boastful; they invent ways of doing evil; they disobey their parents; they have no understanding, no fidelity, no love, no mercy. Although they know God's righteous decree that those who do such things deserve death, they not only continue to do these very things but also approve of those who practice them"*[311].

My point here is not to list categories of sin, but to note that although such people do know the difference between right and wrong, they choose to do the wrong, and furthermore, some even approve of others who do likewise.

When Judas went to the priests and agreed to betray Jesus, we read this in their attitude. Luke 22:5 tells us *"they were delighted and agreed to give him money"*. We need to understand that sometimes (I venture even to think often), sinfulness on our part can trigger delight and approval from those around us AND bring material or some other kind of gain for us. Approval of others does not mean we are doing the right thing.

Humanity / Weakness

This is different to deliberate sin. We all have weak spots, areas where for one reason or another we fail again and again. Paul speaks of this struggle too, he speaks of an inner battle against sin: *"I do not understand what I do. For what I want to do I do not do, but what I hate I do. And if I do what I do not want to do, I agree that the law is good. As it is, it is no longer I myself who do it, but it is sin living in me. For I know that good itself does not dwell in me, that is, in my sinful nature. For I have the desire to do what is good, but I cannot carry it out. For I do not do the good I want to do, but the evil I do not want to do—this I keep on doing"*[312].

This is the experience of many Christians. We fight this battle daily. It is hinted at when Jesus talks about "daily we must take up our cross, deny ourselves and follow him". But we slip and fall from time to time. The good news though, is, we have forgiveness in Christ: *"If we confess our sins, he is faithful and just and will forgive us our sins and purify us from all unrighteousness"*[313].

But realise this, there is a world of difference between falling into sin, realising it and fighting against it, and consciously and deliberately engaging in activity we know is sinful. Or even approving of it.

Direct Spiritual Attack

We must understand that we are in a spiritual battle, Ephesians 6 says this quite clearly, and our enemy Satan does not rest. We read in 1 Peter 5:8 *"Be alert and of sober mind. Your enemy the devil prowls around like a roaring lion looking for someone to devour"*.

It was Satan who entered into Judas. See Luke 22:1-6 and John 13:27 (only occurs here in John's gospel!). We are told in James to *"resist the Devil and he will flee from you"*[314]. How do we do that? How do we resist? How do we keep from sinning? We must recognise what sin is and how it works, we must recognise the attacks when they come. If we understand the characteristics of sin, we have a fighting chance of defending against it.

Characteristics of Sin

In the account of Judas betrayal, there are some lessons about the characteristics of sin we can learn so that we can guard against them ...

Matthew 26v14-16 *"Then one of the Twelve—the one called Judas Iscariot —went to the chief priests and asked, "What are you willing to give me if I hand him over to you?" So they counted out for him thirty silver coins. From then on Judas watched for an opportunity to hand him over"*.

Mark 14v10,11 *"Then Judas Iscariot, one of the Twelve, went to the chief priests to betray Jesus to them. They were delighted to hear this and promised to give him money. So he watched for an opportunity to hand him over"*.

Luke 22v3-6_ *"Then Satan entered Judas, called Iscariot, one of the Twelve. And Judas went to the chief priests and the officers of the temple guard and dis-*

cussed with them how he might betray Jesus. They were delighted and agreed to give him money. He consented, and watched for an opportunity to hand Jesus over to them when no crowd was present"_.

I want to make two seemingly unconnected statements:

1. My big brother is an atheist. He claims that the terms "God" and the "Devil" are just our way of putting substance on Good and Evil.
2. Earlier in my ministry, when doing children's and youth work, we used a parachute canopy that we used for playing games with young children. One of the games they really loved was called "cat and mouse", two or three young children get under the outspread chute, and one of them gets on top. The rest of the kids fan the chute, and the job of the child on top (the cat) is to catch the kids underneath (the mice). It sounds easy, but since the parachute is being rippled, and the mice are trying not to be caught, often the cat has great difficulty in even seeing where the mice are, let alone catching them!.

Do you see the connection? The devil is a great deceiver. John 8:44 says that the devil is *"a liar and the father of all lies"*. He likes nothing better than to convince people he doesn't exist. If you don't believe that he exists, you cannot resist him - he is rippling the chute and hiding his true identity. If we are to resist the devil who the Bible tells us is the prince of the realm of evil[315], we have to learn to recognise him. Here are some tactics he uses…

Sin Creeps in Privately

Most people if asked would say Judas betrayed Jesus in the Garden of Gethsemane, but I would like to suggest that his betrayal happened much earlier than that, in a private meeting with the priests.

1. Gethsemane = public
2. Meeting with the priests = private

Sin doesn't enter in publicly, it comes in the private, in the dark. Sin is not born in front of people, it is there long before, in the private place.

The Bible recognises that people who sin prefer the darkness: *"men prefer the darkness instead of the light because their deeds were evil"*[316].

Sin lives in the hidden recesses of our hearts, where our true character and personality lie. Our public faithfulness to God is rooted in our private faithfulness to Him. . That is why Jesus is the LIGHT of the world. You don't dispel darkness by fighting it, you dispel it by turning on a light. Integrity is about being in the light, with nothing hidden, it is being the same both sides of the front door. Are we one person at work, another when out with friends, and yet another at home? Am I?

Are you? That is hypocrisy, and we know what Jesus thinks about hypocrites!

Even our motivations are not always what they seem — a motive that "cares" for others may not be all it seems. Changing your actions is important, but it is not enough, it's like putting the cart before the horse. It is in the hidden recesses of our hearts that our true character and personality lie.

1 Samuel 16v7 tells us that *"man looks at the outward appearance , but God looks at the heart"*. The light of the world shines His light into our hearts[317].

The bottom line is this one - We DO what we do because we ARE what we are. We don't become righteous and forgiven by doing stuff - we do stuff because Jesus made us righteous and forgiven.

Sin Doesn't Happen by Accident

When did the betrayal happen? - it was NOT at the Last Supper, it was NOT in Gethsemane, it was long before then, it was in the heart and inner man of Judas when he went to the chief priests. This was not an uncharacteristic slip, it was not a man who was trying to follow Jesus and failed in a moment of temper or of weakness. Judas' betrayal of Jesus was premeditated and planned out. We read that after his meeting with the priests, from that moment *"he looked for an opportunity to hand him over"* [318], so we know that:

1. He planned the kiss

2. He planned the location and the time
3. He waited for his opportunity to strike.

Satan is likewise waiting for an opportunity to strike at us. Romans 7:11 describes it like this: _"sin, seizing the opportunity afforded by the commandment, deceived me, and through the commandment put me to death".

How many times do we watch on our TVs or hear people saying - "it just happened, I didn't plan it!"? That is, frankly, CODSWALLOP!! When you don't take care with your character, with who you are, when you don't watch out for and take steps to avoid the pitfalls of life, you are being as irresponsible and reckless as someone who doesn't maintain their car and then claims they are completely innocent when it fails, causes an accident and kills someone.

Guard your heart and your spirit because for every one of us, sin is waiting in the sidelines to grab us, and the battle is not won or lost in the event (whatever that is), it is won in our wills and in our Spirits.

1 Timothy 4:16 tells us to *"Watch your life and doctrine closely. Persevere in them, because if you do, you will save both yourself and your hearers"*.

Proverbs 4:23 says *"guard your heart, for everything you do flows from it"*.

So what is the GOOD news?

God Knows and STILL He Loves

Jesus was well aware of Judas' plans to betray him, yet he still included him in everything he did. Judas was one of the 12 Jesus sent out and who came back with stories of miracles. Judas was one of the disciples who distributed bread and fish to the crowds when Jesus fed 5,000 miraculously. He was one of the disciples whose feet were washed by Jesus and he was served with the bread and wine by the Saviour.

Jesus knew Judas's heart, yet He still washes the feet of the one who has ALREADY decided to betray him. Jesus knew Judas' heart, yet loved him anyway. At the last supper - Jesus ministered bread and wine to Judas BEFORE he left the room to betray him.

This is remarkable if you think about it. It tells us so much about the love God has for us. He knows our weaknesses, he knows our wickedness, yet he still loves us. God knows all we ever have done or ever will do, yet the Bible is clear that *"while we were still sinners, Christ died for us"*[319].

We are told that when Judas left the room, that the disciples thought that he was going out to pay for something. John 13v27ff. *"What you are about to do, do quickly," Jesus told him, but no one at the meal understood why Jesus said this to him. Since Judas had charge of the money, some thought Jesus was telling him to buy what was needed for the Feast, or to give something to the poor.*

The dipping of the bread was yet another fulfilment of Old Testament prophecy that reveals Jesus as Messiah

... John 13v18 describes it as a fulfilment of messianic prophecy - from Psalm 41v9

In Matthew 13 in the parable of the wheat and weeds, the harvesters are told not to remove any of the weeds to protect the wheat. The implication for us is that we must serve everyone, and that at the right time, God will deal with it, he will separate the wheat from the chaff. Let's leave the separating up to God.

He will reveal what is in our hearts - even if not in this world, our hearts will be revealed for what they are when we meet Him face to face.

This is or should be so encouraging for us, that despite ourselves, Jesus knows what we are like and still he offers us salvation and victory over evil - not though our own goodness, but through the cross.

It is through the cross that Salvation is possible, not by our works, or even our proximity to Jesus, but through the very thing that the Devil used to try to defeat Jesus - the cross. When we resist evil, when we flee towards the Cross, we gain the very thing that the devil is trying to take from us, our salvation, and our peace. Now that's Good News!

Our confidence is in the Lord, and we can say, *"The Lord will rescue me from every evil attack and will bring me safely to His heavenly kingdom. To Him be the glory for ever and ever"*[320].

1   Acts 4v13 describes Peter and John as 'uneducated common men'. It is possible that Matthew, being a tax collector, had a degree of education, but in the main, they would not have been regarded as scholars.

2   Luke 18:25

3   Malachi 1:14

4   Malachi 1:6

5   Haggai 1:9

6   Luke 6:46

7   Matthew 6:5, 16

8   Philippians 3v8

9   Luke 18:29-30

10 Luke 18:18-22

11 St Paul is a key figure in the growth of the early church and in the documents of the New Teastament (he actually wrote nearly a quarter of it!). You can read about him in Acts and his letters. He is not one of the 12, though he does call himself an apostle and defends his right to do so. Most notably in the second letter to the Corinthians.

12 Ezra 7:8,9

13 1 Timothy 4:12

14 1 Timothy 4:13

15 Acts 6:2-4

16 John 8:28

17 Matthew 28:19

18 John 13: 12

19 John 13:14, 15

20 Romans 8:29

21 1 John 3:2

22 John 3:30

23 Luke 9:23-24

24 John 1:1

25 John 13:14,15

26 Philippians 2:2-5

27 John 6:26

28 John 6:29

29 John 6:66-69

30 Synoptic, which means "see together" is a description of the gospels of Matthew, Mark and Luke since there are many similarities in the events they record.

31 cf. Matthew 26:73

32 For example, his accent is recognised in Luke 22:59

33 With the possible exception of John

34 John 1:42, 20:15ff

35 Matthew 16:17

36 John 1:44

37 Isaiah 6:5 & Jeremiah 1:1-10

38 1 Samuel 16:7

39 1 Timothy 4:12

40 Judges 6:15

41 Judges 11:1-3

42 John 1:46

43 1 Corinthians 1:28, Romans 4:17

44 Genesis 18

45 Exodus

46 Esther 7:34

47 Acts 15:36-41

48 Matthew 5:9

49 Matthew 26:33

50 Matthew 10:32,33

51 Matthew 26:33

52 Matthew 4:19

53 John 21:19

54 John 1:35-42

55 John 6:8

56 John 12:22

57 *"close eye"* literally means "looked with jealousy and suspicion"

58 Luke 22:24

59 Luke 22:26

60 Luke 22:27

61   Exodus 4:2

62   Matthew 26:11, Mark 14:7, John 12:8

63   1 John 1:1-4

64   Psalm 34:8

65   Revelation 3:20

66   John 4:42

67   John 4:38

68   John 18.15,16

69   Luke 9.53-56

70   Jonah 4:4

71   Matthew 5:21-22

72   Matthew 5:27-28

73   Mark 9:35

74   Matthew 20:26, 27

75   Luke 22:26

76   for example, Ephesians 6:5; Hebrews 10:25; 1 Corinthians 6:19, 31

77   Matthew 22:37-38

78   Ephesians 3:16-21

79   The word hate here is a semitic idiom for "love less". It is a relative term meaning not to honour or privilege something above something else. In other words, Jesus must be the number one priority in your life even above family and your own life.

80   Luke 14:26-27

81   Luke 12:51-53

82   John 15:20

83   John 16:33

84   Revelation 20:4

85   1 Peter 4:14, 16

86   Matthew 5:11

87   Jesus Freak (1995) track: "What if I Stumble?"

88   When I Survey by Isaac Watts (1674-1748)

89   consisting of Peter, James and John

90   Luke 5:10; John 1:44

91   Mark 1:19-20

92   Mark 15:40; Luke 8:3

93   John 1:35; Mark 1:19-20; Luke 5:10

94   Mark 5:37; Luke 8:51

95   Matthew 17:1; Mark 9:2; Luke 9:28

96   Matthew 26:37; Mark 14:33

97   Mark 3:17; Luke 9:54

98   Mark 10:35

99   Luke 22:8

100 John 13:25

101 John 18:15-16

102 John 19:26–27

103 John 21:1-7

104 Acts 3:1-4:22; 8:14-17

105   Galatians 2:9
106   Revelation 1:9
107   John 19:26,27
108   e.g. John 13v23, 20v2, 21v7, 21v20
109   Genesis 2:7
110   Genesis 1:27
111   Psalm 139:16
112   Psalm 139:13
113   Psalm 139:14
114   Matthew 10:30; Psalm 139:4
115   Matthew 10:31
116   Psalm 8:6–8; Genesis 1:26, 28
117   Psalm 8:5; Genesis 1:26
118   John 3:16
119   1 John 4:10
120   Romans 5:8
121   Psalms 144:3-4 (ESV)
122   Psalm 22:6-7
123   Job 25:4-6 (ESV)
124   Exodus 3:11
125   (Exodus 4:13)
126   Jeremiah 1:6
127   Judges 6:15
128   1 Samuel 9:21
129   2 Chronicles 26:16

130   Matthew 23:12

131   Philippians 2:3-5

132   Romans 12:3

133   John 3:16

134   1 John 4:10

135   Ephesians 5:8

136   read 1 Corinthians 6:7-11

137   2 Corinthians 5:17

138   John 19:25-27

139   1 Corinthians 3:10b-15

140   Revelation 2:23

141   Revelation 20:12

142   Revelation 22:12

143   in the KJV at least, the NIV calls them our inheritance, which is a particular form of gift

144   Ephesians 6:12

145   John 19:27

146   Luke 16:9

147   Luke 21:17

148   John 15:15

149   Luke 6:12,13

150   Matthew 15:16 *"Are you still so dull?"*

151   2 Corinthians 6:14

152   James 2:23

153 2 Chronicles 20:7

154 Isaiah 41:8

155 John 15:14

156 John 1:43-51

157 John 1:45

158 John 1:46

159 John 1:46 *"Nazareth! Can anything good come from there?"*

160 John 6:1-15

161 James 1:3-4

162 John 14:8

163 Philippians 4:12

164 Haggai 1:6

165 John 14:9

166 Hebrews 1:3

167 John 1:18

168 John 1:47

169 John 1:50

170 John 1:49

171 John 1:47

172 2 Corinthians 5:17

173 1 Samuel 16:7

174 Romans 11:11ff elaborates on this

175 Ephesians 2:8,9

176 Luke 6:45

177 Proverbs 4:23

178 Genesis 18:25

179 John 1:50

180 Hebrews 4:13

181 Psalm 33:13-15

182 Proverbs 5:21

183 Jeremiah 16:17

184 Jeremiah 23:23-24

185 Daniel 2:22

186 I say "often" as Jesus uses the term "son of man" of himself. Many take this to mean that he is human. This is certainly possible, but is not the only explanation, it could be a reference to the term "Son of Man" found esp. in Daniel which is very clearly a reference not to a man, but to God. cf. Daniel 7:13

187 Matthew 23:15

188 John 1:1

189 John 20:31

190 Ephesians 1:21

191 John 6:15

192 John 3:20

193 2 Timothy 3:16

194 Colossians 2:20

195 Romans 6:2

196 John 20:24

197 Matthew 26:31-35; Mark 14:27-31; Luke 22:31-34

198 John 20:24-29

199 Luke 24:11

200 Matthew 28:17

201 Hebrews 10:24

202 Ecclesiastes 4:9-12

203 1 Peter 1:8-9

204 James 1:6-7

205 Matthew 21:21

206 Mark 9:14-29

207 Romans 10:17

208 Matthew 9:9

209 Mark 2:14

210 Luke 5:27-29

211 Mark 2:14; Luke 5:27

212 Mark 3:18; Matt. 10:3; Luke 6:15; Acts 1:13

213 Matthew 21:31-32

214 Isaiah 44:28

215 Luke 4:24-28

216 John 4:1-42

217 Luke 10:25-37

218 Matthew 8:5-13

219 e.g. Matthew 4:19

220   1 Timothy 6:10

221   Leviticus 19:15

222   1 Corinthians 3:13

223   Matthew 19:21

224   Acts 4:32

225   1 Chronicles 29:16-17 (Emphasis mine)

226   1 Corinthians 8:6

227   Philippians 3:7-8

228   1 Peter 1:7

229   Luke 9:62

230   Matthew 19:21

231   Matthew 10:37-38

232   Philippians 3:7-8

233   2 Peter 3:9

234   2 Peter 3:10

235   Luke 5:29

236   Revelation 19:9

237   Isaiah 25:6

238   Psalm 23:5

239   Luke 15:7,10

240   Mark 16:15

241   Matthew 25:23

242   1 Corinthians 1:26ff

243   Acts 4:13

244   Acts 22:3

245 2 Corinthians 11:6

246 Genesis 25:24

247 Genesis 37:3ff

248 Mark 3:17

249 John 21:21,22

250 Judges 3:12ff

251 2 Corinthians 12:7

252 1 Timothy 4:12

253 Judges 6:15

254 Judges 11:1-3

255 John 1:46

256 Luke 15:11-32

257 Matthew 9:9-13

258 Judges 7:2

259 1 Corinthians 1:28

260 Jeremiah 1:5

261 Isaiah 49:1

262 1 Corinthians 6:9ff

263 Ephesians 2:1ff

264 Romans 4:17

265 James 2:5

266 Philippians 2:5ff (MSG)

267 Luke 10:27; Matthew 22:37; Mark 12:30

268 Romans 12:11

269 Colossians 3:23

270   Revelation 2:4

271   Revelation 3:14-16

272   Matthew 15:8 quoting Isaiah 29:13

273   e.g. Luke 6:27

274   cf. Nehemiah 4:2

275   cf. John 4:9; 8:48

276   Luke 6:27-36

277   Romans 5:10

278   Colossians 3:13

279   Ephesians 4:32

280   Matthew 6:14,15

281   Luke 6:35

282   John MacArthur; 12 Ordinary Men; Nelson Books 2002

283   Matthew chapters 5-7

284   Matthew 15:16-20

285   Jeremiah 24:7

286   Ezekiel 36:27-28

287   Acts 2:37 (emphasis mine)

288   John 6:28-29

289   Romans 10:9, 10

290   Micah 6:8

291   John 14:22

292   Isaiah 55:9

293   Proverbs 14:12

294 Proverbs 16:9
295 John 6:15
296 a quote of Job 7:17 / Psalm 144:3,4
297 Luke 18:9
298 Luke 18:14
299 Romans 12:3
300 Philippians 2:5-8
301 Isaiah 66:2
302 Isaiah 57:15
303 John 14:17
304 John 14:19
305 Romans 1:20
306 2 Corinthians 4:4
307 Acts 10:41-42
308 Revelation 1:7
309 John 12:5-6
310 Matthew 7:21ff., Luke 6:46
311 Romans 1:28-32
312 Romans 7:15-19
313 1 John 1:9
314 James 4:7
315 Ephesians 6:12, Luke 11:18 Matthew 25:41
316 John 3:19
317 2 Corinthians 4v6
318 Matthew 26:16, Mark 14:11, Luke 22:6

319 Romans 5v8
320 2 Timothy 4:18

Printed in Great Britain
by Amazon